Gospel Vulnerability

The Key to Costly Love

Other books by
MARY SHARON MOORE

Anointed for a Purpose
Conformed to Christ
Dare to Believe, Rise Up to Act
Living as Jesus Taught
Lord, Teach Us to Pray
Moving in God's Direction
Nature Notes
Seven Last Words and Eight Words of Easter
Storytelling Our Lives
Touching the Reign of God

Read sample pages and purchase direct on the Store page at
marysharonmoore.com
or, support your local independent bookseller

Request bulk discounts (six or more copies of any title)
direct from the author at connect@marysharonmoore.com

Gospel Vulnerability
The Key to Costly Love

Mary Sharon Moore

AWAKENING VOCATIONS
Springfield, Oregon

GOSPEL VULNERABILITY
The Key to Costly Love

© 2024 Mary Sharon Moore. All rights reserved.

For permission to reproduce any portion of this book or to quote, please email: connect@marysharonmoore.com

ISBN: 9798884778696

Scripture citations noted NAB are from *The New American Bible* (Grand Rapids, MI: World Publishing, 1987)

COVER PHOTO
Mary Sharon Moore

COVER DESIGN
Dan Villani

For all U.S. orders, this book is manufactured in the United States of America with chlorine-free ink on 30% acid-free postconsumer waste recycled material; Forest Stewardship Council (FSC)-certified.

To my fellow workers at the
Egan Warming Centers in Lane County, Oregon

Though termed "volunteers,"
your steadfast commitment to serve
"the least of these" on bitter cold winter nights
reveals the power, beauty, and urgency
of Costly Love in our world today.

You may, or possibly not, "follow Jesus,"
but you walk the Good Road with
firm intention and strong hearts.
I see you. I love you.

Contents

	Opening Words: The Challenge of Gospel Vulnerability	1
1	Vulnerability: Two Definitions	9
2	Embracing the Vulnerable Life	27
3	Gospel Vulnerability: Expression of Radical Trust	41
4	Vulnerability of Core Convictions	55
5	The Prophetic Core of Gospel Vulnerability	71
6	Gospel Vulnerability and the Mission of Costly Love	89
7	Practical Steps to Living Gospel Vulnerability	99
	Closing Words: Why Gospel Vulnerability Matters in Our World Today	111

Opening Words

The Challenge of Gospel Vulnerability

The most intentional, resolute, and consequential choice I have ever made was to follow this man Jesus. It didn't come once in the fervor of an altar call, but in a job interview, and sometime later, in my parked car, when I had plenty of time to think.

These are just two of the stories I share in these pages. I discover that my choice to intentionally and resolutely follow Jesus determines how I spend my time, my energies and abilities, my public presence—daily.

Love strong enough to hold my life together, especially when it falls apart, is what I call Costly Love, the One Love, Love enfleshed. I know this Love as Jesus of the Gospels, who dwells in the hidden Holy One, the GOD of many names, and whose Spirit is my breath. This Love is my sure knowing.

As a writer in the public square, my aim is not to "push a brand" but to open fresh conversations on the power, beauty, and urgency of living Costly Love in our world today. I am motivated by the teachings and radical life witness of this man Jesus.

Why intentionally choose to learn from and follow this convicted troublemaker, this Holy Outlaw? Why? Because he gave *his* intentional and resolute *Yes* to follow the dream, the deep desiring, of this hidden Holy One. He "set his face like flint," as the prophet Isaiah puts it. I strive to do the same.

Each day, each hour, sometimes each moment, places me at the threshold of what is new, untested, unrehearsed, unknown. Daily I sense my innate vulnerability, and this is a good thing. It's a good road I'm on, the Good Road. I'm pretty sure I've seen you on it, too.

You and I, by virtue of our shared humanity, live vulnerable lives. Even more so we who strive to walk this Good Road, or feel at least curious, intrigued, or drawn to walk it alongside others.

Christian faith—seeing as Jesus saw, feeling as Jesus felt, believing as Jesus believed, trusting as Jesus trusted— renders us vulnerable *exactly* at those points where we would much rather feel secure.

I am speaking of a living, dynamic, radical trust which is very different from any neatly wrapped package of doctrines and rituals handed on, too often unopened, unexplored, and therefore insufficiently lived, from one generation to the next.

We search for what is real, because we sense that something inside us is incomplete, waiting to emerge, leap forth, and burst into what w've not yet named, a living flame of Love, all consuming, life-giving, transforming what it touches into the Spirit of the living Christ.

Costly Love, I say, is *outward-facing servant-hearted kinship with another,* with others, which transcends differences and interior resistance. Costly Love carries an impelling sense of solidarity with the other, *for the sake of the other.* Jesus calls this Agape (ä-GÄ-pā) Love which he shares with his followers and commands them also to share (see John 15:9-17; see also 21:15-17).[1]

---

[1] My thanks to David Strahan for reminding me of this powerful word.

Costly Love expresses a selfless *generosity* toward the good of the other. This other may be actual kin to me, or someone I encounter and will never see again. Costly Love is not reserved for the people we like, nor for those who are obviously oppressed. It flows where it will, which is everywhere. This challenges our world of dualities—"the deserving" versus "the foe."

Costly Love is not an expression of "approval" but of deep yearning for the good, the unshackling, the liberation of the other, *every* other, for the sake of their humanity and the healing of the world. This is what Jesus means when he insists: *Love* your enemies (see Matthew 5:44), those whose very existence grieves you.

We do not hear this language, so what does it mean?

Costly Love: Another name for the Buried Treasure, the Pearl of Great Price

Our lives are unthinkingly noisy (which means, also, unthinkingly violent). We build the life that *we* have in mind, the life we've been taught to seek. We also are decent, kind people, willing to respond generously in times of need. It's just that, for the most part, we've been inculturated from an early age, ensnared, you might say, in the sticky web of greedy, grasping King Mammon (see Matthew 6:24; Luke 16:13).

Invitations into real, authentic, wholehearted engagement in life are, in great part, lost on us. We find every reason to *not* dial down the noise, not just yet, not now. We keep a firm grip on the linear, the logical, the measurable, the acquirable. We seem unable to step toward, and even embrace, what is whole-making, costly, that requires handing over everything we have for the buried Treasure, the most sought Pearl, precious beyond all others (see Matthew 13:44-46).

So, to seek out and embrace Costly Love, the hidden Treasure, the costly Pearl, we first must undergo a conversion of attitude and habit, and opt for what reveals the deeper value of our being, our humanity, our meaning and purpose in life. For me, the terms *hidden Treasure*, the *costly Pearl*, and Costly Love itself, are not so much nouns as verbs, not so much things as ways of *showing up in the world* which point us to the hidden Mystery, the Holy One, whom many call GOD.

Jesus: On a mission; therefore, so are we
I speak here of risk, of total, straight-ahead trust, that will cause you to abandon your nets, the tools of your trade, your career path, your carefully crafted plans, your comfort, your many forms of security, because Someone looked into your eyes, ignited your soul, and spoke your name in a way that *changed everything* in your one precious hard-won life.

You step out of the boat in night's darkest hour, in the *midst* of the squall, because the One whom you are convinced will never let you go has beckoned you to *come!*

I'm going to guess that most people, most of the time, can't fully go there. Why? It's *just too risky.*

Getting honest with, and embracing, our innate vulnerability is the key to understanding Jesus. It's the key that unlocks the truth of *his* humanity, *his* vulnerability, *his* vision, *his* mission, *his* way of showing up in an oppressed, unjust, and suffering world, *his* way of girding his heart amid religious oppression, not for reactive violence but in preemptive Love, at all times, straight through to the end, and then beyond.

"Follow me" is Jesus' first, continuous, and also ultimate invitation to us, personally, and together as community—whether we are at the center of community or laboring at its margins. It's an invitation into a lifetime of *willing* vulnerability: to meet this man Jesus where *he* is, to live with a good heart, to walk the Good Road with him, and to love whom and what he loves.

Don't simply *think* about me, he urges; *follow* me. I'm here with you. Walk *with* me.

Jesus: Revolutionary of the heart
Jesus was a revolutionary, living simultaneously at the margins and at the center of a land occupied by Roman rule. But he was not first a political or even social revolutionary. He was a *revolutionary of the heart.*

The word *revolution* is rooted in the word *revolve: re-* meaning "back," and *volvere* meaning to "roll" or "walk." So I picture a *revolution* here as a walking, or rolling, or orbiting, perhaps, around an axis or gravitational center.

With Jesus, this gravitational center is Love, expressed in interior relationship with the hidden GOD, and also in outward-facing relationship of self with humankind and all of Creation.

Jesus' life-as-revolution also was *revelatory,* one continuous unveiling of the Divine, hidden in plain sight, for everyone to see.

Jesus came not to turn things upside down, but to set unjust social arrangements rightside up, in the ways of divine justice, right relations, right action, compassion, for the flourishing of all Creation, including us.

In his great inaugural teaching, in the Gospel of Matthew (chapters 5-7), Jesus speaks not as a preacher with an opinion, but with the soul-shaking authority of a prophet. "You have heard it said …," he cries out; "but *I* say to you …" He speaks with the full force of Teacher On Fire with fresh invitations from a just and loving GOD.

Divine revolutionary Love heals, purifies, and reshapes individual hearts, attitudes, and ways of being in the world—including the world of relationships, and by extension, the social and political order. Which is why it is so important that you and I, today, *show up,* starting close in, locally, to shape and inhabit the Land of the Rightside Up, in the *midst* of the Land of the Upside Down, through acts of justice, integrity, compassion, generosity, and joy.[2]

The challenge? Rearrange your life
In the Beatitudes (see Matthew 5:3-12), Jesus shows us how to engage our hearts with the heart of GOD *in this world.* "Be poor in spirit," he says; "grieve what needs to be grieved; be meek. *Hunger and thirst for justice!* Be merciful, clean of heart. *Be peacemakers!"* he urges. "And don't resist persecution for my sake."

He acknowledges that few are able to actually walk the narrow road with him that leads to the Beatitude life (see Matthew 7:13-14).

To live the willingly vulnerable life in this all-in way, I discover that I need to *arrange my life* around this man

---

[2] I first mention the Lands of the Rightside Up and the Upside Down in my book *Anointed for a Purpose* (Awakening Vocations, 2012), and explore these terms more extensively in *Dare to Believe, Rise Up to Act* (Awakening Vocations, 2019).

Jesus. I need to arrange every dimension of my life around the truth and beauty, the vision, the core convictions, and the daily invitations he offers me to walk *with* him, to go where he goes, and to love whom and what he loves.

I feel an urgency to do this now, to arrange my life *where it is now,* in its present decade, amid these complex times, for the sake of the world I touch, and which GOD still so achingly loves.

I hope you feel this urgency, too, in the here-and-now, as you consider what "walking with Jesus" might look like for *you,* on your courageous and life-shaping journey. I hope to show a way that is simple and beautiful, not complex but challenging, an invitation to Costly Love. May *nothing* hold you back.

In these pages you'll hear five stories and a statement of faith; you'll learn four repeatable steps, and discover endless opportunities to acknowledge, enter into, and willingly embrace your own vulnerabilities in living a life of Costly Love.

Our exploration includes:
1. Vulnerability: Two Definitions
2. Embracing the Vulnerable Life
3. Gospel Vulnerability: Expression of Radical Trust
4. Vulnerability of Core Convictions
5. The Prophetic Core of Gospel Vulnerability
6. Gospel Vulnerability and the Mission of Costly Love
7. Practical Steps to Living Gospel Vulnerability

Each part ends with a takeaway and an assignment: to ponder a thought-provoking question or two, a built-in personal or small group Study Guide.

Shall we go?

Part 1

Vulnerability: Two Definitions

> Though he was in the form of GOD,
> Jesus did not deem equality with GOD
> as something to be grasped at.
>
> Rather, he emptied himself, ...
> obediently accepting even death, death on a cross.
>
> Because of this, GOD highly exalted him ...
> So that, at Jesus' name every knee must bend ...
> and every tongue proclaim to the glory of GOD the Father:
> JESUS CHRIST IS LORD.
>
> see Philippians 2:6-11

These lines of a credal hymn of early church send a bold message to the Roman Empire's nerve center: *This man Jesus,* executed as a revolutionary, an outlaw, in a backwater colony, is LORD. Not Caesar, who claims the titles "Son of God" and "Lord," but Jesus, crucified LORD, yes, and now risen CHRIST.

A bold statement indeed, which tagged his early followers as enemies of Caesar, hurling them into the jaws of bloody persecution and the religious thought police into a frenzy.

This is the form of vulnerability—both political and personal—I wish to explore here. It's a vulnerability we are increasingly challenged to embrace in the cause of nonviolent transformative Justice[3] and an enduring culture of Peace.

Vulnerability is a complex word. So let's begin with some definitions.

What is *vulnerability*?

In its simplest form, vulnerability means *exposure to the possibility of being wounded.* Vulnerability is an essential—*and therefore ultimately inescapable*—dimension of our shared humanity.

Despite all efforts to armor up, we still are enwrapped in flesh. We may stand stoic and unmoved, but the human heart, human emotions, eventually cause us to sway, to weep, to rethink, to change our stand, to break and fall apart. Through the experience we become more real, transformed. We are not too big, too strong, too fortressed, too educated, too credentialed, too privileged, too financially secure, to fail or fall apart. And let's be honest. *Mostly we grow by falling apart.*

Our existence, at every moment, with every breath, is provisional. Just read the daily news, or listen to the stories of a friend, or a stranger. Life, at times, is a wild, scary, unpredictable ride. Your life and mine are far more precarious than we think.

But that's not the point. This is the life which Jesus willingly embraced in the cause of revealing a radically transformative Love, delivering us from our illusions of invincibility.

So, I want to be clear: Vulnerability comes in two forms.

---

[3] My sincere thanks to Cynthia Kokis of Church Women United of Lane County (OR) for calling my attention to this foundational dimension of justice.

Unwilling vulnerability

Unwilling vulnerability is the experience—or at least the prospect—of losing those necessary boundaries between your self and what holds power to harm you, crush you, or completely annihilate you.

Unwilling vulnerability reveals the *uneven match* between brute power, cruel policies, or even random havoc, and a trust that "I'll be OK." Daily, abuse and chaos of every sort reveal the raw injustice of this mismatch. Our society, our world, is saturated and profoundly traumatized with experiences of unwilling vulnerability.

The poor, the weak, those deprived of autonomy and the means to speak and act on their own behalf are unwillingly vulnerable to the life-crushing machinery of systems and social arrangements designed to entrap them and reduce them to easy prey. I call it *power over,* which is the opposite of a fruitful mutuality of power mobilized for a greater good. The arrangements that inflict *unwilling* vulnerability are an abomination in the sight of all that is sacred and true.

At a personal level, skewed religious notions can obscure the tragic dance between a calculating abuser and an empathic, well meaning victim-enabler. Such an arrangement is neither "GOD's will" nor a victim's path to holiness through "sacrificial love." This tragic dance results only in damage to one's self, to one's family, and to the perpetrator of the violence, and needs to be honestly acknowledged. *Unwilling* vulnerability in the home, the workplace, in therapy, school, and church spaces, has so deeply infected our society that we assume that it's something that the powerful will get away with and unwillingly vulnerable others must endure.

Wounding of the *unwillingly* vulnerable, whether by intention or mindless habit, whether through systemic, cultural, or incidental presumption of the upper hand, is an offense against Love, against Justice, an offense against human dignity. An offense against Life.

Unwilling vulnerability has no place at all in the divine plan for just and flourishing relationships within society. By virtue of our common bond, we *must* defend not only the humanity of those victimized, but also the humanity of perpetrators of violence, who are incapable of defending it themselves, broken as they are. This act of radical nonviolent resistance is what Jesus means when he insists: "Love your enemies" (Matthew 5:44).

Willing vulnerability
But there is another kind of vulnerability. I call it *willing* vulnerability, or Gospel vulnerability: chosen, embraced, always outward-facing in service to Costly Love and the divine vision of how life always was meant to be.

Willing vulnerability, in dangerous circumstances or dangerous times, is the willingness to *forsake self-protective boundaries in the cause of prophetic witness*[4] *and justice,* to interrupt the dynamic of violence, to identify with vulnerable others, to stand *with* them, or stand in their place, as Jesus did, and continues to do through people of conscience and good will today.

Willing vulnerability understands the urgency of the times, the magnitude of the need, the imperative to act, and steps forward with courage, humility, compassion, and conviction.

---

[4] I address prophetic witness in Part 5.

Willing vulnerability is an *active intentional entry into places of suffering,* of danger, of inconvenience, or at least into places of not knowing, and possible rejection, in order to interrupt the dynamics of darkness, futility, oppression, death, and to bring light and life, hope, and fresh possibility.

Willing vulnerability is courageous, willing to be *off-center situationally* while being deeply *on-center existentially.* The real center is the unfathomable and ever-surprising Spirit of the Holy One, whether we know, or *think* we know, this Spirit or not.

Willing vulnerability's only purpose: Costly Love

Willing vulnerability is the unifying thread that runs through the four Gospels, distinguishing them from other writings, anecdotes, or "gospels" of the life of Jesus, fascinating though they may be.

Jesus fearlessly danced beyond the well-defined edges of traditional understandings of GOD. And the people who came to hear his teachings instinctively recognized that "he taught with authority, and not like their scribes" (see Matthew 7:28-29; Mark 1:22; Luke 4:32). He took them to a place of astonishingly deeper insight, frighteningly deeper truth, deeper challenge, deeper invitation, in the cause of Costly Love.

Yet Luke tells us that for all their astonishment, his hometown people rushed at this young rabbi to hurl him off the brow of the hill, because he shed light on the limits of their faith (see Luke 4:22-30). He peeled back the religious veneer and exposed their *spiritual* vulnerability.

I'll be honest with you: When you seek to pattern your life on the life of this man Jesus, *willing* vulnerability will define your way of being human, as he was, living justly, humbly, generously, and compassionately among others, especially those who are *unwillingly* vulnerable.

Close-in experiences of willing vulnerability

If you've ever deeply loved someone, you know well that love puts you at your most vulnerable, which you willingly choose because, impelled by Love itself, you know you can choose no other.

I recall, as a child, playing in the water along the public easement at the nearby lake. Perhaps I slip beyond the smooth rocks toward the deeper channel. Suddenly I'm in over my head.

I see a murky light. I try to stand, but my feet can't find bottom. I enter into silent slow motion, and serenely drift, suspended, feeling unexplainably secure, at peace.

Mother—never known to be a swimmer—leaps into the water, fully clothed, shoes and all, and rescues me. Without a second thought she becomes *willingly* vulnerable in the cause of Mother-love for her imperiled daughter, even as the woman sitting on a blanket nearby laughs uproariously at the sight of us returning, my mother drenched and shaken.

My mother, yes, vulnerable even to a stranger's humiliating laugh, as she works to calm her adrenaline-charged heart.

An inconvenient form of Love

Why seek to live in willing vulnerability? Why actively seek a life of Costly Love?

Why? Because the heart of the Holy One is burdened with an aching desire for the divine vision to be our lived reality here and now—on Earth, as in Heaven. I speak not poetically but as one who daily sees the images, as you do, of real and intractable human violence, mean-spirited oppression, carried out with impunity, and the massive human and creational suffering that results from it.

It's more convenient to *not* notice, to switch channels, to unsubscribe. But personal, societal, and creational wounds, unaddressed, simply multiply and fester. Living *willingly* vulnerable in a wounded and wounding world is terribly inconvenient, yet in the cause of Love we can't simply walk away. Costly Love changes us for life.

Willing vulnerability in a world of social privilege
Some forms of willing vulnerability are instinctual. A mother sees that her daughter has slipped underwater, out of sight. Instinct impels the mother to save her child. She gives no thought to strategy or optics. *Just go!*

Other forms of willing vulnerability are *intentional* acts of compassion, of justice and decency, choosing to let go the buffers and *suffer with* the other, affirming that "whoever you are, we are of a kind"—humankind. Here, willing vulnerability breaks through the ever-hardening bubble of social privilege. Social privilege—being born with all the right boxes already checked—may shield me, but only for a while, from having to undergo a life of troubling situations and inescapable social suffering.

Social privilege itself, as we experience it today, is a *manifestation of power unjustly snatched* from the socially vulnerable *many* to the benefit of the socially secure *few*. For those who live inescapably under the thumb of Big Power, the very thought of social privilege rubs the wrong way. Unmerited social privilege is a sign of society's brokenness.[5]

---

[5] Labor unions, which emerged from the Industrial Revolution, exist to confront and transform unjust Big Power arrangements in the workplace.

In cities, towns, and rural regions I see situations of Big Power privilege that are not acceptable, the fruit of predatory arrangements that are rigged and rotten to the core, that offend humanity, that go against conscience, and break the heart of GOD. My own experience of dignity, the stirrings of conscience, and a sense that I can—and *must*—do something, impel me to act in some way to relieve the vulnerability and suffering of those who are powerless, and to address policies and systems, too numerous to count and deemed Too Big To Fail.

I may have the wherewithal, the means, at least *some* means, to intervene and change the situation, or challenge the system. You might say, I have some privilege here, some *agency* to act in the cause of solidarity to achieve just and fruitful solutions. By *agency* I mean the ability, the capacity, to act effectively toward a desired outcome that benefits others.

But privilege, as Jesus experienced it, was not social currency for a protected life. He did not deem equality with GOD "as something to be grasped at" (see Philippians 2:6). Jesus understood "divine privilege" as an *opportunity* to mobilize unexplainable good for the sake of those who suffer. With Jesus, GOD has "skin in the game," and holds an undiminishable divine investment in the flourishing of humanity and all Creation.

Based on Jesus' teaching and example, early church understood social dynamics as radically different from Empire's model: the body is *one,* and the gifts are *many,* distributed for the good of *all* (see 1 Corinthians 12:12-31). The social arrangement was not about social privilege but about intentional inclusion.

PART 1 | VULNERABILITY: TWO DEFINITIONS

A second look at privilege

Let me offer you another way of seeing. You or I may be born into unmerited social privilege, inheriting a sweet deal freely bestowed. Or, we may work diligently, and the desired and even expected doors swing open for us.

But as we mature in our awareness of how society actually works, and grow in our sense of Life's meaning and purpose—not just for ourselves but for everyone, we discover that privilege becomes our *invitation to live life generously,* as Jesus did. He shows us how it's done.

I want to repeat this: Unmerited social privilege is our *invitation to live life generously!* Another word—more sobering—for *invitation* is: *responsibility.*

Jesus teaches his followers: When *you* give alms, don't blow a trumpet. When you distribute *your* goods to others, don't even let one hand know what the other hand is doing. *Focus on the joy of living generously,* he seems to say, and your heavenly Abba who is generous will repay you richly (see Matthew 6:1-4).

I discover a certain freedom here, freedom to *not have to worry* that I will somehow be diminished if I give away some of my self, my means, my security, my time, my freedom, my name, my space.

Now privilege *mobilized* becomes an act of *inclusion,* not exclusion, an outpouring of goods that finds no reason, no desire, to count the cost.

The *real* privilege is to stand as Jesus stood, with the Divine heart beating in our chest, as witness to the divine desiring for a world that is just, compassionate, generous, at peace. We *can* be "living signs of a love that can bridge all divisions and heal all wounds," as twentieth century writer and teacher Henri Nouwen once said.

What might willing vulnerability look like?

A story: "Wheelchair Sister"[6]

It's a balmy summer evening. Friends will be arriving any minute now for a weekly book study.

But what is this? Through my open fourth-floor windows I hear a commotion down below.

I look out and see a woman in a wheelchair taking the blows of a man ramming his folded walker into her wheels. *Not OK,* I think, as I grab my phone and keys and fly downstairs.

By the time I get out the door they have moved from the sidewalk to the parking lot in front of my apartment building. And now another man has joined the fray. The two men are ready to come to blows, with Wheelchair Sister caught in the middle.

Instinctively, I approach and insert myself physically between the two men, my arm, my open hand, outstretched toward the woman.

"How are you doing?" I ask in a firm, clear voice, my eyes fixed intently on hers.

The two men back away, their rage repelled by some seen-though-unseen force. Wheelchair Sister fixes her eyes on me, grasps my outstretched hand with both of hers, and does not let it go.

The second man, still filled with rage, gets into his big white SUV and burns rubber as he peels out of the parking lot.

I turn and see Wheelchair Sister and her companion move toward the sidewalk—she in her wheelchair, he with his walker, walking toward the low evening sun on East 11th Avenue.

---

[6] A version of "Wheelchair Sister" appears in my book *Dare to Believe, Rise Up to Act*.

What was that about? I wonder, as I wait for my book group to arrive.

Notice what you pray for

How easily we say, *Lord, increase my faith!* Which the Lord probably understands as a plea: *Test me!*

If I really want faith, I have to be willing, on a moment's notice, to be inconvenienced, to walk across the *uncertain* surface right before me. And if I want to be a channel of abiding peace, I can expect to be hurled into the midst of conflict.

Yet when the actual invitations arrive—too frightening, too immediate, too challenging, and yes, too inconvenient—how tempting it is to push back, to resist. Perhaps, even, to flee. Or, perhaps, to freeze in place. Or, simply, and very quietly, slip away and hide.

But if I fix my eyes fiercely on the One who calls me, most especially in the perilous night, in the uncertain circumstance, in the undesired season, and walk *into* the Mystery of Love, I become a channel of courage for those who, likewise, are invited to step out of the boat and to walk, with courage, toward the One who calls them, too.

This is not my doing but the work of Love, invisible until it is enfleshed, the work of the One who is Peace, whose Spirit is my breath, whose blood flows in my veins.[7]

I offer you now eight identifying markers of willing vulnerability. These qualities are not linear or hierarchical,

---

[7] My story, "Whose Blood Flows In My Veins" is available on Spotify. The story also appears in my book, *Living as Jesus Taught: Ways of Being Witness in the World* (Awakening Vocations, 2020).

but interconnected, each one shaping and enriching the others, with Willing Vulnerability as their common core.

Eight qualities of the willingly vulnerable life

How do we recognize the willingly vulnerable ones? What qualities do they express?

First, they are clear-eyed and intentional. Willing vulnerability is just that: *an act of will* to forgo self-protection (of time, resources, reputation, personal safety, or what I think defines me) in order to aid or benefit another, or others. The willingly vulnerable see the situation, recognize or at least intuit the risks, discern their capacity to respond, and, with clear mind and whole heart, rise up to act in the cause of Costly Love.

Eight Qualities of the Willingly Vulnerable Life

- Clear-eyed, intentional
- Humble
- Other-focused
- Generous
- Courageous
- Compassionate
- Hospitable
- Nonviolent

The Willingly Vulnerable Life

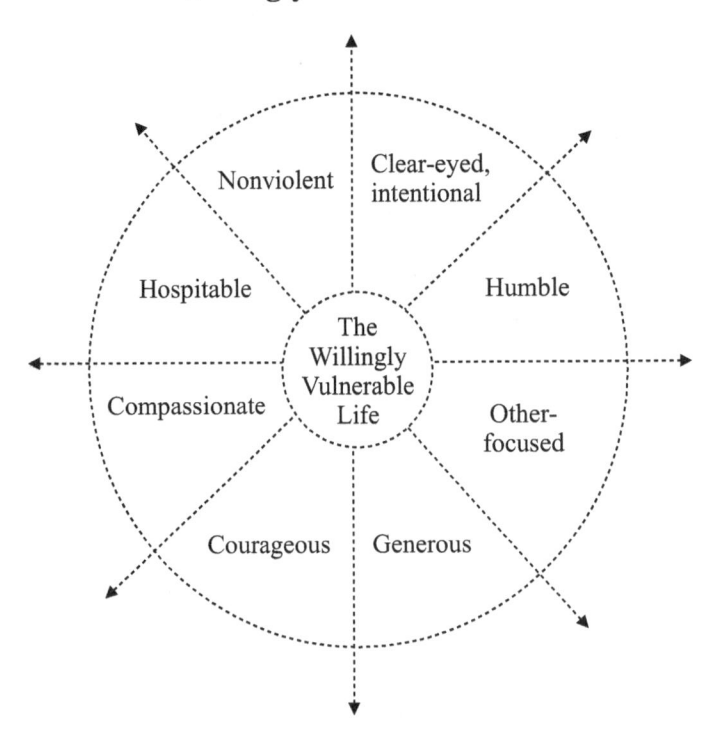

Second, they are humble. They recognize that they could be otherwise (rescuer, problem solver, hero), yet like Jesus, they set aside their claims to privilege in order to mobilize their capacities for the good of others. Free from self-serving ego, they enter, pure-hearted, into authentic servanthood.

Third, they are other-focused. The willingly vulnerable are impelled by the situation of *the other*, the humanity and suffering of *the other*, to bring relief or benefit, or at least to open a space for the other to feel not alone.

Fourth, they are generous. Generosity is the pure instinctive outward flow of the many forms of wealth that come with privilege. It may be the offer of a ride, fresh produce from the garden, or the gift of time and presence; it may be financial generosity, shelter, or forms of accompaniment that call forth the fuller self of the other.

Fifth, they are courageous. Those who live willingly vulnerable for the good of others cultivate strength of heart. They do not retreat in fear, nor stew over all the "what ifs." They act in spite of fear. Knowingly or not, they willingly embrace Jesus' constant admonitions to *not be afraid*.

Sixth, they are compassionate. They are willing to *suffer with* the other (*com-* + *passio*), to get close enough —personally or virtually—to feel something of the other's pain and to accompany or be in solidarity with them in some supportive or healing way. A felt connection, or empathy (*en-* + *pathos*) with the suffering of others is foundational to deep Humanity.

Seventh, they are hospitable. Hospitality, in its broadest sense, means to hold open a space for the other in a welcoming, restorative way. Hospitality draws the other —whether a family member, friend, or stranger—to freely rest a while at the hearth of the heart.

Eighth, they are deeply and consistently engaged nonviolently in their world. The willingly vulnerable defend others against the violence that has saturated every dimension of society, including the small spaces of ordinary daily life, and the hidden spaces of memory, attitude, and heart. They seek to nonviolently preserve, defend, and call forth the inherent good, dignity, and worth within others, doing so sometimes at great personal cost.

Gospel vulnerability isn't a *sometimes* thing I do but a way I strive to be in the world *consistently,* reliably, living compassionately in kinship with humanity—whether close-in or global—and with all of Creation. Hence, willing vulnerability is a lifestyle, not so much chosen as one to which we are continually drawn.

Why nonviolent resistance matters

We today, like Jesus in his time, live in a world soaked in violence, where "power over" sets the terms before the conversation even begins. Indeed, it's not a conversation, not even a debate. "Power over" becomes a nonnegotiable ultimatum. Those who lack power have no seat at the table. They lack the special codes to access the front door, the elevator, the private suite, the restroom.

At his arrest in the Garden of Olives, Jesus points to the futility of meeting violence with violence. "Put your sword back into its sheath," he says to one of those who accompanied him. He adds, as a clear message to his followers: "Those who take the sword will perish by the sword" (see Matthew 26:52; in John 18:11 the one with the sword is identified as Peter). He does not resist the mob who've come to take him away. He stands firm in his truth and his mission, though it means arrest, trial, inescapable suffering, and public execution.

Nonviolent resistance and peacemaking

The word *nonviolence* seems to define itself by what it is not: it is not-violence, not-violation. Nonviolence and peacemaking are related, but one precedes the other. Nonviolence is *the soil in which peacemaking takes root, grows, and bears fruit in right action.* So, I define nonviolence as an *interior disposition.* It becomes the filter for our words, the lens through which we read a situation, and sense a way to perhaps deescalate, or defuse the situation, or to be a healing, reconciling presence in some way, here and now.

Which means: *Nonviolence is a practiced, disciplined way of being in the world.* Nonviolent resistance to the forces of death is a mature fruit of a life lived in the Mystery of Love. As we ardently hope and the Gospels proclaim: Love, not violence, Life, not death, will have the final word.

Peacemaking, therefore, is the *outward expression* of the nonviolent heart, and *always* comes from a place of interior *freedom*. First of all, interior freedom *from* discord, violence, war; it's the antidote to "othering." This freedom *from* is the *purifying* dimension of peacemaking. You become *free from* what clouds your ability to see and perceive rightly.

And *second*, peacemaking is freedom *for* the flourishing of life, *appreciation* of the other; freedom *for* the *protection and advancement* of humanity and the good of society.

Peacemaking acknowledges that we, all together, are of a kind—*Humankind*—and therefore capable of kindness for one another. When a person of deep intentional peace walks into a contentious situation, the exhausting dualities of us-against-them seem to lose their footing, their focus, their traction, their power. Which means: Peacemaking is a *creative and liberating way of being in the world.*

Where Innocence fits in

Jesus speaks a word of caution to his disciples: "I am sending you out like sheep amid wolves: be cunning as serpents, and innocent as doves" (see Matthew 10:16).

Innocence, like vulnerability, has to do with the possibility of being wounded. Innocence is unable to construct defenses against the sharp edges and brutal blows of everyday experience and pervasive injustice.

Innocence is *not* the same as naïveté, which is an expression of simple foolishness, "cluelessness," we might say, living in undiscerning trust. Rather, Innocence *discerns* the situation and *choses* to not go to the toxic side. Innocence does not opt for disengagement. It actively chooses to *not engage on others' violent terms.*

Jesus says that unless we become like *children*— innocent, not engaging in the complications of violence— we cannot enter into the divine ethos, the mindset of profound, abiding peace, the reign of GOD (see Mark 10:15; Matthew 18:3; Luke 18:17). Reclaiming our innate Innocence is a work of interior transformation.

The takeaway

Actual courage in the face of *willing* vulnerability is not something you have to pray for. For those who embrace the willingly vulnerable life, the power of courage is *already given,* waiting to be called into service, in *this* situation, *this* encounter.

And I'll be honest with you. *Especially* in situations that beckon your courageous response, you'll know the *magnitude of the invitation* by the *intensity of the pushback*.

Befriend Brother Pushback, Sister Pushback, enough to ask: *What message have you come to tell me?* This is an important *discernment* question. Do *not* allow fear to have the final word. Probe for the honest answer. Trust your hunch, your intuition, and act as you are led.

The assignment

Ask yourself: What does *willing* vulnerability look and feel like in my life at this time? Where am I willingly stepping out, taking a risk? What's the situation?

And ask yourself: What does this situation *ask* of me? And how am I responding?

What's that story? Shape the story, and share it.

Part 2 explores what it means to walk with Jesus, the Vulnerable One.

Part 2

Embracing the Vulnerable Life

> Jesus began to teach his followers that
> the Son of Man must suffer many things and be rejected by
> the elders, chief priests, and scribes, and be killed,
> and on the third day, be raised.
>
> He spoke these things openly.
> And Peter took him aside and spoke sharply to him.
>
> But Jesus turned around, and looking at the others,
> rebuked Peter: "Get behind me, Satan!
> You think not as GOD does, but as humans do."
>
> see Mark 8:31-33
see also Matthew 16:21-23; Luke 9:22

In Part 1 we looked at two forms of vulnerability: one that is thrust upon those who are *unwillingly* exposed to the possibility of being wounded, the other that is willingly embraced in the cause of justice for the good of another, or others. Now we explore what might be asked of us as we embrace the life of *willing* vulnerability, which Jesus chose.

I wonder if we ever really understand that, when we make our choice to live *willingly* vulnerable in the cause of Costly Love, we choose a precarious, dangerous, and even Righteous Outlaw way of being in the world, a way that cannot settle for play-it-safe compliance with unjust social arrangements.[8]

---

[8] In Parts 3, 4, and 5 I identify Jesus as Holy Outlaw, Righteous Outlaw, and Prophetic Outlaw.

I wonder if we ever consider what it means—what might be asked of us—to actually *follow* the Righteous Outlaw, to burn our gaze, as Jesus did, through unjust laws, through oppressive and humiliating social, legal, and religious norms deemed too sacred to be questioned.

I wonder, in the two millennia span of Christianity, how many sermons, how many public teachings through word or action, have been prophetically delivered, courageously received, and put into action.

A few, I'm sure. Especially in times of persecution, war, or civil unrest, and at great personal risk. Salvadoran Archbishop Oscar Romero would know, as would Rev. Dr. Martin Luther King, Jr.; Holocaust victims Edith Stein, Maximilian Kolbe, and Etty Hillesum; advocate of Brazil's poor Sister Dorothy Stang, India's Mohandas Gandhi, and countless others.[9]

Precarity: It's not in my dictionary

I first came across the word *precarity* in the writings of Catholic Worker co-founder Dorothy Day. She will not mislead you on the tremendous sacrifice and constant material uncertainties of a life lived in Costly Love.

So, I look up *precarity* in my *Webster's New World Dictionary*. It's not there. The closest word, *precariousness,* sounds a little less ... stark. *Precarity,* however, has a sharp and prickly sound. Precarity sounds inescapable because, well, it is.

My online search, drawing from Oxford Languages, tells me that precarity is "a state of persistent insecurity with regard to employment or income."

---

[9] While Gandhi was Hindu, he openly embraced the teachings and challenge of the radically nonviolent Jesus, especially as presented in Matthew chapters 5-7; for this witness he eventually underwent a tragic and violent death.

I say it's a state of persistent insecurity with regard to *everything related to your sheer existence* in a world full of unpredictable, uncontrollable, inhospitable, and often malicious forces. Precarity moves us quickly from our isolated sense of self-sufficiency to the necessary mutuality of community, even the community of strangers.

Precarity lies at the core of the life of Costly Love. The mystical writings of the Apostle Paul affirm repeatedly: *Our lives are not our own: they belong to Christ.* And Jesus says: If you want to follow me, get ready to shoulder your cross. We'll be doing some dangerous Outlaw work.

Precarity: An expression of Poverty of Spirit
The provisional nature of humanity and the persistent insecurity of all living things are forms of *poverty*. When *willingly* embraced, and even *preferred* for a greater good, they become "poverty of spirit," which Jesus says is a blessed way to be. Like him, we strive to accept our innate poverty and the limitations of our existence, not with *reactive* self-preservation but with *proactive*, preemptive Love. Jesus did precisely this. He shows us how it's done.

Through the ages, spanning continents and cultures, in public places and in the close-in, homely spaces, countless others have embraced lives "poor in spirit," whether they would name it that or not.

To willingly embrace a life of precarity in service to Love means to let go illusions of self-sufficiency, power, inflated ego, air-tight security. Sadly, even tragically, I'll say, "Christian" is too often seen as a precarity-proof brand. But actually following the precarious Holy Outlaw way is a commitment worthy of our solemn *Yes*. We will will be tested—privately, publicly, by those close-in, and by those who despise us from an amplified distance.

Jesus sent the Twelve on a mission to teach and heal in his name, with clear instruction: Take nothing with you but a walking stick: no food, no money, no backpack, no sandals. In Mark's account they *can* wear sandals, but cannot bring a second tunic (see Mark 6:8-9; see also Matthew 10:9-10; Luke 9:3; 10:4).

Would I leave home to go teach in this Holy Outlaw's name without credit cards, phone, laptop, chargers, and proper ID? Yet I have traveled and taught in his name dragging my smart-looking, well-packed roller bag through airports, wearing my favorite western wear boots and a touch of bling. Travel and lodging? That's all set up in advance by someone else.

No precarity here. From the looks of it, I live far from the vulnerable path. It's just the practical, prudent thing to do these days, right?

Jesus' identity and mission: No buffer against precarity
Mark's account of Jesus' first prediction of his impending arrest, suffering, and death is preceded by a probing identity question: *Who do people say that I am?*

His disciples offer various answers: John the Baptizer, Elijah, one of the prophets.

"But *you*," he asks more intimately, more directly, "Who do *you* say that I am?" Maybe he wants to hear their honest declaration of commitment as all-in disciples.

The Teacher may want to know: Have you been paying attention? Do you *see* the power of GOD at work? I ask *you:* Who do *you* say that I am?

Following, perhaps, an uncomfortable silence, Peter speaks up: "You are the Messiah, the Christ" (see Mark 8:27-30). Right answer, wrong understanding.

The long-awaited Messiah is supposed to save the people from oppression, not be publicly executed under false testimony of his adversaries and the heavy hand of the state. Yet in this moment, Peter and the others have no idea how badly shaken they will be by events in the very near future.

Hence, Jesus' paradox of what's coming: If you want to save your life, he warns, you'll lose it. *If you lose your life for my sake and the sake of the gospel, you'll save it.* And Peter won't have any of that (see Mark 8:31-33).

Jesus offers no triumphal road here, but the dusty, contested, dung-caked path of willing vulnerability, in service to Costly Love.

My identity and mission: No buffer against precarity
Starting, I notice, with my intentional, resolute choice to follow this man Jesus, my life becomes not-my-own. I opt for a mission not of my choosing, yet of my deepest desiring. And I'll be honest with you: I live this choice inconsistently, at times timidly, poorly, yet with earnest intention to grow into it more wholeheartedly.

My allegiance is to the One with the nail scars, the willingly vulnerable One, who not only *teaches* me but *shows* me how to live and die generously, faithfully, in order to be transformed through my consistent, nonviolent, and wholehearted embrace of it all.

I have learned, and often say, that if I want to follow Jesus, I have to go where he goes, and love whom and what he loves. What does this phrase really mean: to go where Jesus goes, and to love whom and what he loves?

Early intuitions of the vulnerable life

On high school spiritual retreats, I remember hearing that Jesus meets me where I am. Well, I think, I've been experiencing this meeting since about the age of eight. So please, *tell me more*. But I don't recall hearing "more." I heard consolation and encouragement, but not really challenge or invitation, not as I stood at the threshold of my young adult life.

Sadly, I slipped into young adulthood understanding an unspoken subtext: Even in the messes I am making in my life, Jesus meets me where I am. The good news? I don't have to hoist myself up out of these messes and clean up my life in order to meet Jesus. I mean: to actually *encounter* him in a way that changes everything, especially my incoherent sense of meaning and purpose.

Surely, there must be more.

What's asked of me?

More is asked of me, or at least *should* be asked of me, if I seek to walk with a Holy Outlaw. I call it: intentional apprenticeship, work-hardening for the mission ahead. I call it: choosing to *not* separate myself from social suffering. Why? Because Jesus gravitated toward those who suffer, especially those at the fringes, under the predatory grip of Roman Empire and the hawk-eyed vigilance of religious authorities.

Why undergo the disciplines of apprenticeship? the rigors of work-hardening, and shedding the protective veneer of social privilege? Why? Because the world in which I live is gasping for the breath of divine imagination and the actions of enfleshed, compassionate, just, and merciful Love, whether the world can name this desperate yearning or not.

So I wonder: What *does* religion ask of me? For the most part, I think: not much. But, I wonder: What does this beckoning divine vision ask of me, enmeshed as I am, like everyone else, in the bruised, broken, and bleeding here-and-now?

Sleepwalking is not an option
I'll be honest with you: I can easily sleepwalk through these days of great suffering which many people undergo, because I'm not losing *my* home to wildfires or floods, typhoons or hurricanes, civil wars, deadly international military operations, genocide. The water I drink is pure, the food abundant, and the soil in my neighborhood is not drenched in toxins.

I'm good. My life is all pretty good. But more is asked of me than sleepwalking through these days. I know in my bones that the time for sleepwalking is over. It's time, *now,* for us to awaken from our "sleep of inhumanity," as Latin American theologian Jon Sobrino puts it.

I need a religion that openly tells me that the time for sleepwalking is over, that I urgently *need* to *believe* the Teacher, and act in ways that contribute to liberation of the world's suffering poor, along with their oppressors. I need a religion that is willing to live what it teaches.

My common-bond humanity tells me the same, in its own urgent language, if only I would rouse myself enough to wake up, pay attention, be changed, and be helpful in some way.

The contested conversation of religion and society

I think of two terms which are contested in our complex 21st century: *religion* and *society*. Both words, both realities, still have a heartbeat, so we still have work to do: to notice, to think, to imagine, to be challenged, and to bring religion and society into dynamic and helpful conversation, for the sake of humanity and all of Creation.

Religion (in Latin, *religare,* to bind together, as in binding one's self to the Divine) comes most fully alive within community, as we find in the Hebrew and early church scriptures, and in Indigenous and other sacred texts.

And *society,* the result of movement from the solitary self and family unit into fellowship of common cause with others, occurs when we recognize that we *need* each other, and that a greater good results when we pool our talents, gifts, experience, and best interests for a greater purpose than we could ever achieve on our own.

Again, I ask myself: What does my *religion* ask of me, and of my engagement in society, in the bruised, broken, and bleeding here-and-now?

My answer must be whole and not selective; all-embracing, not preciously curated. My engagement in *society* (being bound to humanity) must reveal the core of my *religion* (being bound to GOD). And my religion must insist on the intrinsic value and creative life-affirming potential in my bond with society.

So, my concern here is actually following this man Jesus—Teacher, Healer, Righteous Outlaw, crucified Lord, risen Christ: to walk with him on the path of willing vulnerability, which he pursued with all his heart, in service to the Land of the Rightside Up.

Walk with Jesus, the Vulnerable One

If I want to follow Jesus, well, it helps to know: Where *does* he go? Where is he most likely to be found? The Gospels show me clearly and consistently where he's most likely to be found: *among those who suffer.*

Yes, sometimes he's found dining at the tables of the rich. But that's likely after a day in the hot sun, along the dusty lanes, dodging camel dung, teaching the crowds, encountering and touching this one, healing that one, challenging another, tending to their many forms of stinking poverty. Even at the tables of the rich, he sees *their* suffering too, masked behind façades of gold.

In the starry nights he's most likely to be found out beyond the edge of town, absorbed in prayer, out where wild creatures howl and roam. And sometimes he's found at the table of friends who refresh him and nourish him, share stories with him, put him back together.

Following Jesus is a *personal* journey. And for me, what's the point of the journey? It's to make a life's work of loving whom, and what, Jesus loves. It's a lifelong pilgrimage of heart, mind, attitude, and spirit, as much as a journey of miles from here to there.

Bring sturdy shoes and a bottle of water, yes. But more importantly, *bring the totality of who you are,* because daily you will be learning from the Master how to truly love the Lord, your GOD, with all your heart, soul, mind, and strength, and your neighbor as yourself (see Matthew 22:37-39; Mark 12:30-31; Luke 10:27).

Embracing the vulnerable life, the life not of *power over* but *abiding with,* is an intentional act of heart and will, an openness to being *interrupted* by the needs of the moment, the social and moral needs of the times.

Embracing the willingly vulnerable life is an energized response to an irresistible invitation of the Spirit of the living Christ to enter into, and more fully reveal, the Land of the Rightside Up, in this moment, this situation, this life.

What "embracing the vulnerable life" looks like

So then, how might you choose to live a *willingly* vulnerable life, especially if you have access to some degree of power and agency in your world? How do you mobilize your privilege, as Jesus did, in order to live generously in ways that benefit others? What is the *process* of opting to live vulnerably, and perhaps more meekly, on the Earth?

Let's be clear: You do not really *choose* the willingly vulnerable life. The *willingly* vulnerable life chooses *you,* because it is intimately shaped by, and in service to, your unique mission in life—a mission you also do not choose but to which you awaken and embrace. You might start with a hunch, an unbidden glimmer of insight, an intuition, even a restless knowing, rooted in the here-and-now, that life is more than consuming and satisfying your every whim, more than careening from one little splurge to the next, "just because."

Sadly, *choosing* has become a consumer word, a "desired lifestyle" word. *Embracing* the outward-facing vulnerable life in the cause of Love is a wholehearted response to the invitation to live life generously, for the sake of others, not counting the cost.

Embracing the outward-facing vulnerable life implies a willingness to stay awake, to pay attention to what in the world, in *your* world, is going on. It means filtering your sources of information, analysis, and insight *through the lens of the Gospel* and letting go of the rest.

Jesus lived inside the deep conversation between his vulnerability—both unwilling and willing—and the mission of his nonviolent and passionate heart. We hear this conversation in his times of testing in the wide-open wilderness and in the close-in Garden of Olives—at the beginning and toward the culmination of that mission.

He refuses to use power for his own benefit, opting instead for faithfulness and humble, courageous obedience to the confines of his human circumstance and mission. He shows us what such faithfulness to mission might look like in our lives: not using privilege as a fallback or buffer, but accepting the frighteningly provisional nature of being human, and empowered in the Spirit, among other human beings, in their fragile, exhausted, needy, yet precious lives.

A statement of faith

Some years ago a statement of belief flowed from this insight into the provisional nature of Jesus' life, and the provisional nature of my own. I call this statement "I believe Jesus,"[10] and I share it with you now.

> I believe in GOD. I believe in Jesus.
>
> And of course, I believe in the Holy Spirit.
>
> But I find it easier to believe in Jesus. He calls us friends. Yet I instinctively draw back from the presumption of such closeness.
>
> Still, he puts the invitation out there. Delivers it, directly, to my heart.
>
> I deeply believe *in* Jesus—Teacher, Healer, Prophet, Son of the Most High, fully given to his mission of Costly Love.
>
> But, do I *believe* Jesus?

---

[10] This piece can be found as a spoken-word track on my YouTube channel.

To actually *believe* Jesus demands of me an audacity of faith, which impels the audacity of action. I must audaciously *dare* to believe him, or just go away.

Something shifts when I move from asking myself: Do I *believe* Jesus? to stating clearly: *I believe him!*

I am *free* to accept the invitation to go where he goes, to live by the same moral compass, to love fiercely with the same divine love.

I am *free* to wonder what this means, and *free* to take the next step. I am *free* to be led by a curiosity at the core of me that impels me to go beyond myself.

I *believe* Jesus when he says, to me: *I am the Resurrection, and the Life.*

And I understand that resurrection comes after I pass through the many forms of dying.

When Jesus says to me, as he once said to Peter, *"Come,"* I am *free* to lean with all the weight of my being into his invitation.

As he did with Peter, he bids me to hoist myself out of the boat of all that is predictable, and familiar, and comfortable, and safe. He bids me to walk toward him, now, across new uncertain surfaces.

Why? So that I can be where he is, and go where he goes.

Taking Jesus at his word is not complicated, unless I make it complicated with all the reasons why I can't, why it's impractical, why it's not the right time, or just too risky.

But I take him at his word. And therefore I am *free* to rise up in joy, and *free* to act.

Free to believe. *Free* to be changed. *Free* to rise up to act.

Freedom is not a word usually associated with vulnerability. In fact, we usually want to be free to run *from* vulnerability.

However, refusing to participate in, and even creatively, nonviolently *resisting,* unjust systems, and working to relieve oppression and suffering, are courageous, prophetic, and therefore costly actions. In my experience, real courage lies not so much in believing *in* Jesus as actually *believing* him, actually going where he goes and loving whom and what he loves. I mean courage to not just say *Yes* to his teachings but to *upend and reshape my life* in order to experience in my own flesh the beautiful and just desiring of GOD, even in the midst of the mess.

The takeaway
Willingly embracing the vulnerable life for the sake of the Gospel is a decisive moral act, an embodiment of divine generosity.

For Jesus, embracing the vulnerable path to Jerusalem was no mere choice: it was an imperative. He *must* go to Jerusalem, suffer greatly, undergo a public criminal execution. He sets his face like flint.

You don't have to seek out or plan the journey. The journey presents itself, through a hunch, an intuition, a suggestion that arrives, sometimes like a blazing invitation, sometimes quietly, but always as an unquenchable flame of divine Spirit. The invitation happens where you are, *now;* not elsewhere, nor elsewhen. *Believe* the Teacher, the Holy Outlaw. Take him at his word. He is counting on you. He is looking at you now.

The assignment

Ask yourself: Where do I intentionally embrace the vulnerable life, for the good of another, or others? In my family life? my work life? in my community? in civic engagement? What stories come to mind?

And ask yourself: Who or what impels me to embrace this vulnerable life? A role model? a teacher? an experience? a challenge from a mentor? my sacred scriptures or other inspired texts? How might I describe what I am learning?

That's your assignment. I want you to carry it out.

Next, Part 3 explores the radical trust that lies at the core of Gospel vulnerability.

Part 3

Gospel Vulnerability: Expression of Radical Trust

During the fourth watch of the night, Jesus came toward them, walking on the sea. When the disciples saw him ... they were terrified. *It is a ghost!* they cried out in fear.

At once, Jesus said to them: "Take courage! It is I! Do not be afraid!" Peter said in reply, "Lord, if it is really you, command me to walk to you across the water."

And Jesus said: *Come!* Peter got out of the boat, and began to walk to him, on the water.

see Matthew 14:25-28

In Part 2 we explored what it means, and what it takes, to willingly embrace the vulnerable life in following Jesus. Now we explore the radical trust that allowed Jesus to live as Holy Outlaw in service to Costly Love.

We'll examine the root of the word *radical* in its dynamic Gospel context. And I'll invite you to find stories of such willing vulnerability as expressed in your own life.

I have used the terms *willing vulnerability* and *Gospel vulnerability* interchangeably. I want to focus now specifically on Gospel vulnerability, which forms the core of our understanding of Jesus.

Gospel vulnerability is shaped distinctly by Jesus' teachings to his disciples, by his actions of healing and bringing the dead back to life, his sharp-witted nonviolent resistance to those who challenged his authority, and his ultimate nonviolent witness to Costly Love in the course of his arrest, mock trial, scourging, and public execution.

All three synoptic Gospels (Matthew, Mark, Luke) spell out the conditions of discipling with Jesus.[11] These conditions make for sober reading.

Jesus: Holy Outlaw
If you want to walk with me, Jesus says, you have to deny *yourself*. Let go of *your* vision, *your* plan; take up *your* cross (the Roman tool of non-Roman outlaw execution), and follow *me* (see Matthew 16:24).

The synoptic Gospels affirm Jesus' insistence: If you want to follow me, let go of your life, your family ties, your good name and reputation, and the esteem of others. Become a holy outlaw, as I am Holy Outlaw.

He warns: Do not buy into the false securities of the keepers of the Law or Empire's status quo. If you try to preserve your life in that way, I assure you now: You will lose it. And if you let go of your life, your good name, reputation, and the esteem of others *for my sake,* you will save it.[12]

Why? His answer is simple: His only mission is the expression of Costly Love, which gives Spirit, Life, and true meaning to everything.

Wow. With Jesus, it's personal. Am I ready to follow an Outlaw? an outspoken critic and bold resister of religious thought police and Empire's heavy-handed

---

[11] See Matthew 10:37-39 and 16:24-28; Mark 8:34-38; Luke 9:23-27.

[12] See Matthew 10:39, 16:25; Mark 8:35; Luke 17:33. John presents the conditions of discipleship in agrarian terms: "Unless a grain of wheat dies, it remains a grain of wheat. But if it dies, it produces much fruit" (see John 12:24).

regime? He speaks unflinchingly, as one who knows, accepts, and is fully committed to his fate.

The logic of the Gospel: The logic of Costly Love

Yet Jesus' focus is not so much on his eventual fate as on the fire that burns right now in his manly chest: to establish the Land of the Rightside Up in the *midst* of the Land of the Upside Down—not starting with the powerful, the rich, and the influential, but with the lowly who lack agency; not elsewhere but *here,* not elsewhen but *now,* in this nothing-special place which Caesar has colonized to exploit its resources and labor, and harvest its revenues to fill his coffers in Rome.

This Jesus is the One I choose to follow? How about a quiet, low-profile life where I just mind my own business?

The logic of Gospel vulnerability removes *me* as the center of my life and fills that void with the One who *is* Costly Love. If you want to walk with me, Jesus seems to say, be willing to be completely transformed. Choose, he seems to say, as I have chosen, to be hollowed out, purified, readied, and sent for a work that will be larger than you.

Yet Jesus never coerces, just as he was never coerced. The life of Gospel vulnerability is *willingly* embraced from a place of interior freedom and deep commitment to live generously, justly, even sacrificially for others, in this world which GOD still so loves.

We'll be roughed up, misunderstood, and rejected, as he is, he promises, if not by the law, at least by those who think they know us, because the world's powers are not ready to let go a logic of fierce resistance to anything that threatens their perceived legitimacy or stands in their way. The world's powers are not ready to live disarmed, vulnerable, exposed. Generosity apart from tax write-offs and naming rights is not in their business plan.

Yet Jesus speaks a fiercely challenging line to his disciples, to us, when he says: *"Love your enemies. Pray for those who persecute you, and withhold from you the goods of Heaven"* (see Matthew 5:44).

Counterintuitive? Yes, if you think like a citizen of some earthly Empire. To *not* hate the enemy is to betray your tribe. But *loving* your enemies and desiring their good is the path to wholeness and holiness for those who yearn, as Jesus does, for the Good Way, right here, in this place, in this time.

Pray, he says, *for those who persecute you.* This is the foundational logic of the Gospel: radically nonviolent citizenship in unjust and deeply compromised spaces.

Persecution is an unfreedom, a stark violation of personhood—both of the one who is persecuting *and* the one who is being persecuted. Jesus is unwaveringly clear in his teaching: His disciples have no right, no freedom, to return violence for violence, whether in thought, word, or deed. His injunction to "love and pray for your *enemies"* is the injunction to live Costly Love.

Stripped of violence as a fallback, we will feel vulnerable indeed, with nothing to support us, no way to defend ourselves, save through the power of a nonviolent heart. Jesus never tells us: *Don't defend yourselves.* He simply insists that we do it *nonviolently.*[13]

Jesus, Peter, and radical trust
The Gospel story that has held me fast for over twenty-five years is the account of Jesus and Peter

---

[13] My thanks to peace activist and writer John Dear for this insight.

walking on the water (see Matthew 14:24-33; I suggest you stop at the end of verse 29).[14]

Jesus doesn't presume to play the divine card, and he doesn't do magic. So what's going on in this scene?

Matthew's chapter 14 opens (vv. 1-12) with the account of Herod's deeply regretted order to have the imprisoned John the Baptizer beheaded. When Jesus hears of John's death, he gets in a boat to go to a deserted place, no doubt to grieve the loss of his forerunner, his buffer, and to tremble over his own impending fate.

The crowds get word of Jesus' whereabouts, and anticipate his arrival on the far shore. They are sick, tired, and hungry, so Jesus tells his team to feed them. But his team lacks the means, so Jesus provides for the multitudes himself—though he also lacks the means (vv. 13-21).

Bone tired, he dismisses the crowds and his disciples, and finally goes up the mountain, alone, to pray (vv. 22-23), to process this troubling turn of events, to weep, and to lose himself in the consolation of prayer.

Now, I imagine, completely absorbed in prayer, he walks down the mountain, out to the open space, where the land becomes shoreline, and now open sea.

Absorbed in prayer, he walks, vulnerable to the forces of night and the storm on the sea. Vulnerable, as well, to the demands of his mission and the fire burning in his heart. Vulnerable to the magnitude of his unconditional *Yes*. And vulnerable to the unstoppable roll of political

---

[14] Verse 30, where Peter looks down and falls into the waves, easily becomes a laugh line, which excuses us from acknowledging that Peter, for a brief moment, *steps out in radical trust;* and it dismisses the personal invitation to our own mature trust and courageous action.

events and his adversaries' plots for his arrest and execution, over which he has no control.

Now come Peter and his mates in the boat, exhausted and terrified, when they see Jesus walking toward them late at night in the squall. At once, I imagine, Jesus snaps out of his reverie and says: *Take courage! It is I! Do not be afraid!* (v. 27).

Peter, discerning the spirits of this deep-night scene, cries out: "Lord, if it is you, command me—*command* me—to come to you across the waves" (v. 28). And Jesus says: *Come!* (v. 29a).

Peter fixes his eyes on the One who calls him, the One who knows his limitations yet loves and trusts him. And Peter hoists himself out of the boat and begins to walk toward his Lord (v. 29b).

Peter's moment is ours also
In this moment, both stunning and chilling, Peter instinctively looks down at the waves, powerful enough to pull him under. *He takes his eyes off the One who calls him.* He goes under.

Jesus *immediately* catches him and asks the searing question: "What made you doubt me?" (v. 31).

What made you doubt me?

It's not a shaming question but a teacherly one, addressed to a disciple, an apprentice. Jesus could have said: *What made you think I am not worthy of your trust? that I would call you out of the boat only to allow you to drown?* But the wise Teacher keeps the focus of this learning moment on the disciple.

Peter offers no reply. Yet this is the single most important question we can ever be asked of our own actions and interior life. *What made you doubt me?*

The honest answer might be: *The magnitude of the storm, and the alarming depths of my human vulnerability.* Good. The Teacher can work with that.

We sense the magnitude of Jesus' invitation, here embedded in a storm, by the intensity of our pushback. The sooner we become aware of the pushback, the sooner we can let it go and move forward with the invitation.

And the point?
Each invitation to walk on the uncertain surface in our own lives, when we act on it, *flows back* to its Source as an offering of Love. The point of radical trust in Jesus is always the revelation of Love.

Let this phrase settle into your heart, your mind, your attitude, your imagination: *The point of radical trust in Jesus is always, always, the revelation of Love.*

Those who seek this life of Gospel vulnerability discover that they are existentially *incapable* of making safety their first criterion for discernment. This depth of trust is the *radical dimension* of Gospel vulnerability. Considering self-safety is part of human instinct. But the point here is this: We respond to the Teacher's invitation *despite* the risks and dangers. This is called *courage*.

That pesky word *radical*
The word "radical" can feel scary. It may suggest "out of control," or "radicalized," suggesting a sudden, irrational and frightening force. When you start talking or acting "radical," it pretty much guarantees that you will be

Unliked, Unfriended, and dismissed from circles of easily discomfited family and friends.

The word's Latin root, *radix,* means *root,* the deep-lying source of stability, vitality. In agriculture, think of taproot vegetables like carrot or camas or radish. The root is the hidden source of nourishment for the plant's life system.

Similarly, in our context *radical* means: to be firmly established interiorly in the deep soils of meaning and purpose, in order to provide vitality and stability of purpose and action.

The Gospel, for followers of Jesus, is *radical:* it's the taproot, the hidden yet vital root source of life for Christian community. The Gospel itself, when read, pondered, ingested, and enfleshed, is powerful nourishment, powerful medicine. It transcends fleeting rationales, logics, political stances, opinions, and favored notions.

The good news which Jesus preached remains powerful nourishment, powerful medicine for our own lives, for our communities of meaning, and for the world we touch. It supplies necessary interior strength to see clearly, perceive rightly, and to act courageously, justly, creatively, nonviolently, in the cause of wholeness, compassion, transformative Justice, enduring Peace.

Missed opportunities for radical trust
Social and interconnected beings that we are, we know, deep down, that we are accountable to others, for their good, their safety, their humanity. In very real and tangible ways we are our brother's keeper, our sister's kin. We'd want them to see us in this same way, wouldn't we?

In times of trouble? When we find ourselves unwillingly vulnerable? Here I fail the test miserably.

Like the time I'm walking past a fenced school yard on a Sunday afternoon. Children are playing. I sense that a young girl is being lured into a predator's car, engine running, in the middle of the schoolyard.

What can I do? I can't scale the chain link fence, and I'd feel awkward making a loud distracting noise. *Maybe I'm misreading the situation,* I unhelpfully think, *or maybe it's her dad.* And I keep walking.[15]

Or like the Christmas morning when I ardently pray, *Lord, let me see your face,* as I prepare to leave soon to serve a community dinner for folks downtown at noon. And within hours the Lord *does* reveal his face to me. It's translucent pink and puffy, skin grafted and stapled together on the face of a man standing stiffly, painfully alone, in the doorway of the dining hall. Stunned, I turn away.[16]

Radical trust in Jesus, the willingly vulnerable One, is the antidote to my fear, *only when I let it be.* At some point, deep-rooted trust in my Teacher is a choice. Not because stepping out of the boat onto the uncertain surface is a natural act. It's not. But because he alone can bear the full weight of my fear as I choose to trust his call.

His trust in you and me, too, is radical, total, and eventually, for us, utterly transformative. He wants us to *not* turn away, because the Righteous Outlaw counts on us to stand confidently, courageously, in his place, in the world we touch.

---

[15] From "Listen for the Lord," in *Touching the Reign of God*, pp. 26-29.

[16] From "Let Me See Your Face," in *Touching the Reign of God*, pp. 44-48.

Gospel Vulnerability: The Key to Costly Love

Radical trust, radical mercy, to the end

This radical and positive expression of vulnerability, certainly as Jesus models it on the night of his arrest, asks the sobering question: *In the cause of Love, how far are you willing to go? Are you willing to drink the cup? Yes? Down to the dregs?*[17]

Jesus doesn't get stuck in the blinding injustice of his betrayal, arrest, the midnight trial, the merciless flogging, and humiliating march uphill to his public execution. He transcends the injustice of the wounds inflicted on him by those wounded others. He opens his heart in radical compassion, and ultimately transforms their "power over" into a plea to his Abba: *Forgive them. They know not what they do* (see Luke 23:34).

We urgently need to do now as Jesus did in his time: *transcend* the urge to respond to cruelty with cruelty, and *transform* it with forgiveness and Love. Take in the injustice, as Jesus did, the malice, the mean and bleeding spirit of a world drenched in violence, and breathe out Love, merciful, unexplainable Love, purifying Love, no-exceptions-and-no-strings-attached Love.

Jesus *lived* this Costly Love. His every act of transforming *violence received* into *Love returned* was his apprenticeship to his final hour, pinned to the wood, exposed, humiliated in death on the gibbet. This radical trust *is* the fiery core of Gospel vulnerability.

Gospel vulnerability: No calculated risk

Living vulnerably in witness to Costly Love always seeks the good of the other—even when that other is the source of your wounds. This doesn't mean invite the sucker punch. It means stand firm in your humanity, with

---

[17] See Matthew 26:39; Mark 14:36; Luke 22:42.

Love, and defend the humanity of the other, even in their brokenness. Embrace your jailer, as Nelson Mandela did.

Gospel vulnerability can never be a "calculated risk." It's your courageous step in radical trust, when you walk, in dark night, toward a beckoning Love. It's the step that you and I would rather not take, the step we'll find *any* excuse *not* to take.

The ways that you and I express such vulnerability may not be on Peter's epic scale. You and I will never be Peter. But you and I *will be invited,* I assure you, to take our own decisive radical steps in our intention to follow the beckoning One, to go where he goes, to love whom and what he loves—perhaps most especially in the hidden places, the neglected spaces, in the time of storm, and dark night. Or, perhaps, in the light of day.

So I invite you, right now, to take a breath, and reset your heart, mind, and spirit toward that firm intention of courageous humility in the cause of Costly Love. Set aside the urge toward prudence, the urge to calculate the risk, the urge to delay.

What might this decisive and disciplined step look like? Don't start with the epic leap. Start close in. Begin to trust *exactly where you are.* Begin to trust that your life will get rearranged. Here's a snapshot of how this step might go.

A story: "Byebye Bijou"[18]

> So, at the moment, I'm sitting in my car in the shade of a tree near Campbell Community Center.
>
> The engine has just died. Again.

---

[18] This story appears in *Living as Jesus Taught*. The spoken-word version is on my album *Free to Be Free*.

So I have plenty of time to think. About an hour, actually. It usually takes close to an hour before the engine will start again.

Trust me, I know. My car engine dies, a lot.

So I begin to think of all the places my beloved Bijou has inconveniently dropped anchor ...

At the intersection of Willamette and 29th. At Willamette and West 11th. At the South Side Post Office. At East 27th and High Street. In the parking structure beneath the public library. And in Mapleton, at the west base of the Coast Range, where Highway 126 turns a sharp left toward Florence. An isolated place.

The problem is: Bijou is 25 years old, and I take her to the dealer for repair. I should know better. The dealer keeps her for maybe four days, always over a weekend, and to keep me happy he hands me the keys to a current model sweet little ride, thinking I might get hooked on that New Car Smell.

So I think these thoughts as I sit in the shade of this tree at Campbell Center. I turn the key in the ignition, just hoping, but Bijou still isn't starting. So I think some more. I think of how, just last week, I paid my annual auto insurance premium. And how my insurance goes up 20 percent each year, apparently just because it can.

And the question pops into my mind: *Would my world unravel if I didn't have a car?* My eyes drift into middle space. In this moment, I notice, I am free—utterly free—to imagine my life differently.

Where do I go where bus lines do not go? And I have to admit: Nowhere. Well, I may have to walk a few blocks. So what? I can walk a mile in twenty minutes easy. I hike mountain trails for six hours once a week.

I reach for my phone and call my insurance agent. I tell her that I just paid my annual premium, that my car isn't worth it, that I'm going to donate it to charity and I'm not going to replace it. And, might I please get a refund?

The insurance lady is gracious and very understanding. A full refund, of course, she says.

> I am stunned at what I have just said: *I am giving away my car and I am not going to replace it!*
>
> As though I have just uttered a vow to the heavens, I feel my words become like some massive door which swings open, inviting me to Just Walk Through.
>
> My car was freedom to me, until it became an unfreedom. Now I will depend on public transit. I used to drive around with no passengers, totally free. And now I will ride around with fellow passengers, totally free to encounter my world in new ways. I exchange one vulnerability, I notice, for another. *And this is life.*
>
> These are all my people. This is all my community. If I want to follow Jesus, I have to go where he goes, and love whom and what he loves.
>
> Now, a few days later, I bid Bijou adieu as she gets fastened tight on the flatbed of Froggy's Towing truck. I shall not look in the rearview mirror. Rather, I look forward to finding Jesus, among other places, on public transit.

Radical trust? You bet. But first, I ask the towing team for a ride down the hill to the post office. Donating my car to charity and choosing to not replace it was the start of my intentional transition to living a life that enables me, in some ways, to walk and mingle with Jesus and his poor.

The takeaway

Donating my car to charity, and choosing to not replace it, I discovered, is Gospel vulnerability in action—the most important spiritual act of my adult life. I could not have planned this step. When the invitation arrived, I simply did the next obvious thing. I picked up the phone. I made the call. I canceled the policy. I said *Yes!* And I have never looked back.

In that moment, this Holy Outlaw called my name across the water. He calls your name, too. Your invitations will be unique to your life, as mine are to my life. You will be invited to do things you have not yet imagined, things you cannot do apart from the Spirit living in you now.

The assignment

Ask yourself: What courageous and decisive actions have I taken in my adult life, in the cause of Costly Love, that express radical trust? Was it turning down a lucrative job offer to pursue work that aligns with my real mission in life? Was it leaving a steady paycheck to provide long-term care for a family member? Or perhaps some other risky step that has set me free to live generously for the good of others?

And ask yourself: What was this experience like for me? What fruit does it bear today? How have I been changed? What stories come to mind?

Acknowledge and express gratefulness for the courageous steps you take, perhaps even radical steps, perhaps daily, which express your willingness to live vulnerably, as the Holy Outlaw did, in the cause of Costly Love.

In Part 4 we explore the nature of willing vulnerability in our core convictions.

Part 4

Vulnerability of Core Convictions

> If you love father or mother more than me,
> you are not worthy of me.
> If you love son or daughter more than me,
> you are not worthy of me.
> And if you do not take up your cross and follow me,
> you are not worthy of me.
>
> If you find your life, you will lose it.
> And if you lose your life for my sake, you will find it.
>
> see Matthew 10:37-39
> see also Matthew 16:24-25; Luke 14:26-27

Part 3 described the nature, the look and feel, of radical trust, the only kind of trust Jesus ever expressed. It's no leap into foolishness but a step decisively taken in response to the invitation to walk, courageously, onto the uncertain surface of your life now. Invited, as Peter was, by the One who beckons.

Part 4 guides us down to the engine room, to the place of deep convictions that impel us to live willingly vulnerable lives, as Jesus, Righteous Outlaw did, in service to Costly Love.

If you love father or mother, son or daughter, *more than me,* Jesus says. ... If you do *not* take up your cross, he continues. ... If you *find* your life, he says.

The Teacher challenges the life arrangements we take for granted. He cuts to the core.

I feel the sting of his words every time I read them. They are the words of a man who has undergone the disciplines of initiation into the divine vision for life here on Earth, words of a man whose burnished heart is inseparably mixed up with the heart of the hidden yet very present Holy One.

These are the words of the work-hardened Righteous Outlaw, living free of the illusory compromises of the politically colonized, and the smug self-assurance of the religiously secure. Jesus, Righteous Outlaw, lives free of the constraints of the inward-facing life; living not for himself but for humanity in all of its particulars. He lives free from the lies of power and exploitation; free to call forth the dignity and beauty of all Creation and the blessed flourishing of Life.

Jesus: Righteous Outlaw
This man Jesus, Righteous Outlaw, lived with the inescapable core conviction that the Good Way, the reign of GOD, here and now, is possible, *amid* Roman occupation, colonial exploitation, and the unjust and oppressive constraints imposed by the ever-vigilant religious authorities.

Unlike the self-enriching authority of Caesar and his power minions, Jesus' authority is of a completely different quality, scope, and mission.[19] He challenges religious leaders, too, who keep the goods of Heaven under lock and key.

Jesus is clear about his mission, and he expects his followers to single-heartedly share the passion of his core convictions. He insists that they free themselves of

---

[19] "My kingdom is not of this world," Jesus says to Pilate during his trial (see John 18:36). Pilate and Herod, outpost extensions of Caesar's power, were fascinated and perplexed by this nonviolent yet powerful firebrand.

familial and social constraints, and be willing to pour out their lives for the work of countering the status quo with the astonishing inbreaking of the just and beautiful Land of the Rightside Up.

And building the Land of the Rightside Up *within* the walls of the Land of the Upside Down is in-your-face, positively subversive work. It's deadly dangerous work: maybe not to the point of shedding blood, but be ready, the Teacher cautions, to shed whatever holds you back.

If you put tribal identity and blood relations ahead of me, the Master says, *you are not ready to follow me* (see Matthew 10:37; Luke 14:26). He cuts hard to the core. And now he speaks like a mad man: *If you do not take up your cross and follow me ...* (see Matthew 10:38; Luke 14:27).

Positively subversive and deadly dangerous work, when carried out in steadfast nonviolent conviction of the Good, carries a price. *You will be tagged Outlaw,* he assures his followers. *You will dance, as I do daily, at the edge of crucifixion.*

Jesus' nonviolent and positively subversive agency

In the Spirit of this Righteous Outlaw, we *have* agency, as he had: consistent, radically nonviolent yet positively subversive agency. Jesus never was out to "get the enemy." More than anything he wanted to draw "the enemy" into the divine embrace of Love. By all measures, this deep conviction and way of showing up was both Radical and Outlaw, and carried a heavy price.

For Jesus, *positive subversion* is the nonviolent front work that eventually results in *radical inclusion* of even the most stubborn elements of the Land of the Upside Down into the Land of the Rightside Up. It's a form of "wooing with Love." We aren't there yet. We still have work to do that will exceed our lifetime, just as it exceeded his. We work anyway.

Subversive: Sly and subtle

Subversive is a sly, subtle word. In its positive sense, it means *to nonviolently undermine established powers,* to break, not people, but the *cycles of attitudes and actions* that block the flow of Justice, and the flourishing of Life. It means undermining those powers that work *against* the Good, by means of dynamic agency *for* the Good, using actions that circumvent the status quo or reveal its hollow façade.

Positive subversion holds the humanity of the "other," the *adversary,* intact. Positively subversive agency liberates the other to choose the righteous way.

Jesus subverts the powers of violence, injustice, and death with the power of acceptance, forgiveness, and expressions of Costly Love, even in his last hours in the agonies of crucifixion. His teachings present a startling, consistently nonviolent, subversive social dynamic that's radically different from what his followers expected and his adversaries could accept. For this, he was publicly mocked as a failure.[20]

The Teacher slyly subverts his adversaries' "power over," and teaches his followers to do the same: You slap my right cheek? Here's my left. You, Roman soldier, want me to carry your load for one mile? Let's go two. You need to crucify me? Look in my eyes. I tell you: I *forgive* you.

---

[20] John's Gospel notes that the chief priests were displeased with Pilate's inscription on the cross: "Jesus the Nazorean the King of the Jews." They wanted him to write "that he said, 'I am the King of the Jews'" (see John 19:19-21 NAB). In other words, just another failed messiah.

He shows us how consistent, nonviolent, and positively subversive agency for the Good is expressed: Show up in Love, and don't go away.

Clear-eyed, clear-hearted, compelled
To follow this man Jesus, then and now, means to stand in unarmed resistance to unjust cultural and earthly powers. It means choosing to live Costly Love, even to the point of death.

In Jesus' time, crucifixion was the price that non-Roman rabble-rousers paid for stirring up the locals to challenge the powers of Empire. This form of public execution stripped away the humanity of the convicted, and offered a public spectacle designed to both provoke mockery and instill fear among the colonized. It was the preferred way to suppress rebellion and coerce compliance with the prevailing political arrangement. Let the one, the few, serve as a warning to the many.

So the phrase "take up your cross" means that you and I must be ready to accompany this Righteous Outlaw on his mission of Costly Love.

Do you see what he's doing? *He's training us in nonviolent civil disobedience.* And we'd better be ready to shoulder the crossbeam, without whining or backing down, on our march up the hill.

Let go of your *distractions,* this Outlaw seems to say. Let go of your *excuses*—both the lame and sincere. Let go your fear of nonviolent righteous resistance, or fear of nonviolent noncooperation. Let go your *reasons why* now is not the right time, and why this path is not the one you had in mind. *Let go the logic of your well-crafted plans. Let it go!*

Cutting close to home

But when Jesus starts challenging family ties and the expectations of kinship? Perhaps he cuts a little too close to home. At least, it can feel that way.

Jesus surely loved his family and kinfolk. He grew up among them; talked, worked, and relaxed with them, broke bread with them. He knew them, and was known by them.

But at age 12, something changes during his time with the elders in the Temple. His words to his distraught father and mother are revealing: "I thought you would know to look for me here, in my Abba's house, doing what he sent me to do" (see Luke 2:49).

Wow. At age 12, he already is separating from family and forming his core convictions, even as he listens to and questions the respected teachers of the Law.

In the reign of GOD, Jesus seems to say, blood ties can never come first; social and societal expectations can never come first. Indulging in the perks and pleasures of life—*mammon*—can never come first.

Leave all of that. Let it go! Follow me! the Righteous Outlaw says.

Mission in service to Costly Love, he makes clear, is thicker than blood, far thicker than any social norms, or wants, or expectations. Any life you "find" will be too small for you, the Teacher says. If you *let go* the illusion of "finding" your life, you will be free to *receive* the life I yearn to give you (see Matthew 10:39).

Still, family has a place

Yet two chapters later in Matthew's Gospel, as Jesus sits teaching among his disciples, his mother and brothers show up, looking for him. When Jesus learns that they are there and asking for him, with a generous sweep of his arm he says:

> Who are my mother? my sisters? my brothers?
> *Whoever does the will of my Abba* is mother and sister and brother to me. (see Matthew 12:46-50)

Family makes sense *only* in light of the larger mission of Costly Love. Jesus *enlarges* family loyalty to a unified purpose, a shared loyalty to the work of GOD's life of transformative justice, generosity, healing, and joy. Families, he affirms, indeed have a mission.

This mission of Costly Love, rooted in core convictions, is the only mission that really makes sense in a world we would willingly choose to live in.

What you "deeply believe"

Core convictions are the driving force, your taproot, your North Star in troubled days and dark nights, enabling you to navigate your perilous way across the uncertain surfaces of *your* life, *your* work, *your* relationships, and the larger obligations of being human, a part of community, a part of society, in *these* times.

I'm not pointing to some epic life, here, but to rich meaning in common everyday life. Most of us do not live on the world stage. Most of us are not household names, not even in the towns where we live. Many of us are unknown to the folks three doors down from us.

But every one of us has capacity to do small things, the overlooked things, the seemingly inconsequential things, right in front of us, with meaning, and purpose, and intentional Love which remains the most powerful force in the universe.

Core convictions appear in seed form in the small things. I may have a core conviction that my talents and abilities have a purpose, and enable me to be useful in this world, even though others may think I should pursue a more practical or financially secure path.

I may have a core conviction that expressions of Costly Love and transformative Justice are possible in the world I touch. I may have a core conviction that I somehow *must* be, and *will* be, a part of that possibility.

Core convictions are an *interior driving force.* They override, or at least challenge, my preferences for what's convenient, predictable, or safe. Core convictions are what I trust deeply enough to allow them to rearrange my heart and shape and direct the course of my life. They are what I trust deeply enough to risk being inconvenienced, ridiculed, even wounded, in the cause of Costly Love.

Core convictions are invisible, until they're not; intangible, until they become the actions I take in the interior or outer worlds which I inhabit. Core convictions accept no substitutes. They lead me, in surprising and fruitful ways, into new forms of community, in places and ways I would not have imagined.

Loss of a loved one, for example, or loss of any of my own capacities, may lead me to encounter, love, and journey with others on a similarly challenging road. Community forms. We discover that we all need each other. Even those who are not at all like me may have something to teach me, a way to bless me.

Discerning your core convictions

The hardly noticed dance between receiving the invitation—*Come!*—and walking *with* this man Jesus, or *away* from him, or holding back in the boat, will reveal to you where your core convictions lie. Your *pattern* of response to Life's invitations reveals your core convictions: not what you *profess* to believe, but what you actually *give* of yourself wholeheartedly, or not, in response.

The invitation often arrives in subtle ways: a hunch, a chance encounter, a word, a door opening to an unexpected opportunity. Sometimes it's a series of nudges, a pattern of opportunities. Receiving the invitation requires us to slow down, pay attention, notice things—something we're not very good at doing, to our great loss, in the hurry of a scan-and-scroll life. Sadly, being *wholeheartedly present to the moment* is seldom asked of us in our culture today.

Jesus pointedly asks his closest followers their core convictions about him. He's trying to build a tight team, a movement, because he knows his time is short. At one point, many followers drift away, back to their more linear, more predictable, less demanding life. He turns to the Twelve and asks: *Do you want to leave me also?* (see John 6:67). His question, an expression of profound humility, opens him to the possibility of being wounded by their reply.

Jesus lived and taught his core convictions, unfettered by how they might land on others' ears or minds or hearts. Still, the conversion rate, from anonymous crowd follower to committed disciple, was understandably low. Why? *He asks too much!*

Jesus: Out of his mind

Twice in the Gospels Jesus is viewed as being "mad," crazed. In the first instance, Jesus comes home, and so many people show up looking for him that it's impossible for his family even to eat. They try to seize him from the crowds, convinced that "he is out of his mind" (see Mark 3:20-21).

In the second instance, Jesus speaks of the Good Shepherd (see John 10:1-21) who guards the sheep from strangers and false teachers (read: the Pharisees). He describes himself as the sheep gate, as the good shepherd. "I *know* mine, and mine *know* me," he says—something the Pharisees cannot claim with similar affection. Thrown into a dither, they exclaim that he is "possessed and out of his mind. Why pay attention to him?" (see v. 20).

Jesus is existentially incapable of living or teaching otherwise. Why? Because he lives and preaches what he knows and believes *with all his heart:* the divine vision, the reign of GOD, is *possible!* The reign of GOD, which is everything that the reign of Caesar, or the reign of the Pharisees, will never be.

At the trial that led to his crucifixion, Jesus is asked by Pilate: *You are a king?*

Jesus replies, clear and simple: "You say I am a king. For this I was born, for this I came into the world, to testify to the truth. All those who belong to the truth hear my voice" (see John 18:37). Wow. He's *not* out of his mind. He's in full possession of his identity, his purpose, his core convictions, even in the presence of Great Power.

Something within *us* knows how much weight *we* are willing to press to meet the urgencies of *our* times with Costly Love, transformative justice, genuine compassion. Something within us knows the distance we're willing to go in witness to the One who held the world's brokenness in dynamic tension with his vision of the reign of GOD.

Like Jesus, we also have to get "out of our minds"—those places of logic, calculation, and sensibility—and into the places of spine, gut, heart, hunch, *conviction* that the divine vision *is possible,* here, now. All that's asked of us is to give GOD something, *something,* to work with.

The vulnerability of core convictions

On the Good Road, core convictions hold the truth about the deeper, noncommercialized, nonmonetized purpose of humanity; and how we might be a people committed to the good of all within society and all of Creation—in relational, life-giving, nontransactional ways.

Many people who resigned from their jobs in the wake of COVID-19 began to understand, with a deeply disquieting clarity, that their lives were worth more than what they were required to pay, in exchange for the inadequate wages they were receiving.

Life is more than this, they seemed collectively to say. Many had the courage to act on that core conviction, and took the costly yet liberating step of walking away to *imagine their life differently.*

They became free *from* what enshackled them, and in so doing became free *for* new challenges of meaningful and worthy work and creative expression to revitalize their personhood.

Jesus puts it this way: "Is not life more than food and the body more than clothing? Look at the birds in the sky. ... Are you not more important than they?" (see Matthew 6:25-34).

Well, yes, we are, we like to think. Yet sometimes we seem unwilling, unready, to courageously lean into the core conviction that unnameable divine Mystery is the hidden wellspring of our sustenance. None of us can simply "make things happen," like a new job at a worthy wage, nor anything else that might give our lives substance and meaning. But by following a hunch, pursuing a lead, getting out of the boat to take that first courageous step, true to our core convictions, we live the homely proverb: *Begin* to weave, and GOD will provide the thread.

Invited to something more

We *can* give ourselves *wholeheartedly* to meaningful labor, worthy investment of heart, mind, soul, and physical strength, especially in the cause of justice, compassion, creative nonviolent resistance, and divine generosity and joy. We *can* trust that there will be daily bread, and provision for our needs. What we *thought* were needs may become purified, simplified, melted away as excesses of the Land of the Upside Down.

The Apostle Paul knew well the vulnerability of living his core conviction—that Jesus whom he had persecuted was now the risen Christ and worth living for. Under the growing shadow of his own impending death, he pours his life into this conviction (see Galatians 2:20).

Honoring your core convictions by acting on them happens in the particulars, where what you most trust is true will be challenged. Action based on your deepest convictions will leave you vulnerable—sometimes financially, or relationally, sometimes reputationally, and often existentially. This comes with following the Righteous Outlaw.

What might *you* look like when you live your core convictions? Here's what I looked like, once.

A story: "My Family Thinks I'm Nuts"[21]

My assignment, this morning, is not a pleasant one.

Short of running a load of laundry, I can't think of any more chores to distract myself from the work I do not want to do.

The work? Preparing for a job interview.

It's come to this: I need steady employment with a predictable paycheck. I hate to admit it. But the itinerant preacher in me is chewing gravel.

"Get a job, any job," I recall my savvy and caring siblings saying to me after a work assignment had ended. But I cannot shake this desire to live openly, precariously, in service to GOD.

My brothers think I'm nuts.

So to honor their advice I float my resumé, and pretty quickly I'm offered an interview. For a job. In a collections agency. As executive assistant to a Very Busy Young Man who is General Manager.

I'd be at his beck and call, it turns out, 24/7. Not just during the expected ten- to twelve-hour-a-day office shift, but by pager at all times.

"You know," the young man says, "just in case, when I'm golfing with a client in Japan, I might need something."

I feel my eyeballs roll to the back of my head as I sit with this Busy Young Man, and his human resource director, at the agency's enormous and highly-polished conference table.

"And we are pleased to offer you $26,000 a year," he tells me, full of confidence that I will snap up the offer. And pretty confident, too, I'm sure, that at my age I probably don't have any other job offers pending.

Which, it turns out, I don't. Besides, given my impressive executive support experience from earlier

---

[21] The spoken-word version of "My Family Thinks I'm Nuts," on my album *Free to Be Free*.

days, his offer is a ridiculously paltry sum for the demands of the job.

So I allow his offer to hang in the air as I go inward to compose myself and gather just the right words.

"I am not able to accept your offer," I say calmly, my eyes fixed on his. Pause. A significant pause, really.

"I am a woman of Christian faith," I say, "and no job can be the center of my life." I pause again. "Jesus is the center of my life."

The young executive shifts in his chair, sits a little more upright. He clears his throat. The human resource manager is dead quiet, not moving. She's not even breathing.

"Well," he says, "no one has ever spoken to me this way."

Pause. And I am thinking: *Well, I just did!*

"And I respect," he says, "what you have just said."

We rise, shake hands, I thank him for his time and wish him the best. He wishes me the best.

I am already assured of the best, I think, as I walk, with my heart free, right out the door.

Right now he may be thinking I am nuts. Or just plain dreamy-eyed. Too connected to my convictions to appreciate that he had Just Offered Me A Job.

Jesus was sneered at for *his* core convictions, even as he hung on the cross.

What will I do in the cause of Love? What will you do?

I wonder what has become of that busy young man. Perhaps he's still playing golf with his far-flung clients. Perhaps he's had a smooth glide along his career path.

Perhaps he has wrestled with his own core convictions, like Jacob, who wrestled in the night with the mysterious divine messenger (see Genesis 32:23-33).

Perhaps, like Peter, he has heard the irresistible invitation to leave the security of the boat and to walk across the uncertain surface to the One who speaks his name in an irresistible way.

Your core convictions simplify and clarify what you can give yourself to wholeheartedly. And living wholeheartedly is the point of the Great Commandment: Love the Lord your GOD with *all* your heart, soul, mind, and strength; *and,* in exactly the same ways, treat your neighbor.[22]

That neighbor may be a low-wage factory worker in a far-away country, a family fleeing violence in the night, or someone on the street who can't get their life together.

The takeaway
When I chose to *not* work 24/7—sure, for a steady (though underwhelming) paycheck, but also in support of someone else's career aspirations—I discovered Whose mission has the only real claim on my short and precious life.

When you live—really *live*—your core convictions, you learn the inner workings of a life of radical trust. You discover an unimaginable and unapologetic freedom to follow the One who *wants* you to enter into his mission, his companionship. In doing so you step free of the burden of making a life for yourself, and step into the life that actually has your name on it.

---

[22] See Luke 10:25: The Greatest Commandment, and the accompanying Parable of the Good Samaritan (10:29-37), a broadly recognized story of Costly Love.

The assignment

Discerning your core convictions is no guessing game. Find the *patterns* of what most deeply engages you, what gives you joy—or at least a quiet satisfaction, or sense of purpose and fulfillment—*and* that in some way blesses or benefits others. What's the one thing you can't *not* do, can't just ignore or walk away from, because it so deeply expresses who you are?

Core convictions seek outward positive expression through *your* particular skills, talents, gifts, and unique ways of being present. Look for the patterns, acknowledge them honestly, give thanks for what already is happening, and be open to next invitations.

Be on fire. Walk humbly, with courage. Give thanks.

In Part 5 we explore the prophetic dimensions of Gospel vulnerability.

Part 5

The Prophetic Core of Gospel Vulnerability

> Blest are you when they insult you,
> and persecute you, and utter every kind of evil
> against you, because of me.
>
> Rejoice and be glad,
> for your reward will be great in heaven.
> Thus they persecuted the prophets before you.
>
> see Matthew 5:11-12

In Part 4 we looked at the vulnerability of core convictions. When we acknowledge and shape the trajectory of our lives by those convictions, we willingly embrace their vulnerabilities and costs. Why? Because we know, at this point, that we can do no other.

In Part 5 we explore Jesus, Prophetic Outlaw, and the prophetic dimensions of living Gospel vulnerability.

Jesus' inaugural teaching, which Matthew presents in chapters 5 through 7, lays the foundation for entirely new ways of being with GOD, with others, and being in the world with compassion and justice, truth and joy.

Among his followers I see heads nodding *Yes* as he names the blessed ways of being human in this world, until suddenly the language becomes ... unsettlingly *personal*.

"Blest are *you*," he cries out, "when they insult *you*, and persecute *you*, and utter every kind of evil against *you*, because of *me*."

What? I want to follow you, but can't I stay with the meek and mourning piece? Maybe just be merciful and pure of heart, and call it good?

We delude ourselves when we try to construct a smoother road than the one the Teacher is on. The prophetic core of Jesus' vision demands that we be *all in,* with him, in the arduous and sometimes dangerous work of building a just world that works for *everyone,* building the Land of the Rightside Up, in the *midst* of the Land of the Upside Down.

The unjust forces of Empire today are no more *for us* than they were *for him.* Institutional religion itself gets rattled when the prophets come around.

Prophetic justice: A public revelation of Love

Prophets *do* cause a rattle, particularly around social and power arrangements that serve the few at the cost of the many. The most pernicious cost is loss of the rightful and necessary flourishing of humanity and of all Creation.

What does Justice look like through the prophet's lens? I define Justice as what Love looks like in the public spaces, just as Mercy is what Love looks like in the hidden spaces. *Justice is Love made public.* Justice, seen through this lens, is both *restorative*—restoring what has been denied, stolen, or crushed—and *transformative,* for both the denier and the denied, the robber and the robbed, the crusher and those crushed by the heavy boot of raw, totalizing power.

In other words, *prophetic justice is liberating* for both the oppressor *and* the oppressed. This is what it means to "love your enemy." It's Jesus' vision, and it's what fires up the hearts of prophets today.

The *motivation* for justice which restores and transforms is Love. The *process* of such justice is Love. And the *fruit* of restorative, transformative justice is Love. For the prophet, if it's not about Love, it's not about Life. The prophet's taproot is Love.

Prophetic justice affirms and defends the dignity and flourishing of *every* person and *every* element of Creation. Which means: Prophetic justice *invites* perpetrators *and* sufferers of injustice into a better conversation. The very opening of the Book of the Prophet Isaiah spells out Israel's injustices, and then the Holy One says, through the prophet, "Come, now: Let us set things right" (Isaiah 1:18, NAB). What an amazing invitation into a fresh start.

The caution? *Prophets, expect some pushback!*

Jesus: Prophetic Outlaw

Like the prophets before him, Jesus' goal wasn't to be a troublemaker. In the sacred traditions, prophets are *lovers of the Holy One,* lovers of the people, and lovers of Truth so blinding that most people cannot see it.

The Prophetic Outlaw is so named because of a deep-rooted resistance to the unjust ways established and maintained by unjust systems. Unjust practices are *baked into* political and religious institutional systems and social arrangements, *baked into* many city charters, and state and national constitutions. Unjust practices are *enshrined* as inviolable rights. Who can contest them? Well, Prophetic Outlaws do just that.

The Prophetic Outlaw is not a rebel but a Lover; not a ranter but a wooer of the errant, and a healer and restorer of the crushed. Which means: Prophetic work does not start with naming injustice. It starts with *coming close enough to suffer with (com + passio)* those wounded by the many forms of injustice to their humanity.

As Prophetic Outlaw, Jesus drew close to the pain, felt the pain, called out the cause of the pain, and leaned into the power of divine Justice and Mercy to restore and transform broken lives.

Jesus, Prophetic Outlaw, continues this work today, through the *willingly* vulnerable ones who bear the prophetic mantle in our times. Think of Archbishop Romero: Before he was assassinated, he was speaking political truth to his flock, which set him in the cross hairs of those who hated his truth telling.

Think, too, of rights activist Dorothy Stang: Before she was murdered she was defending the Brazilian rural poor from criminal gangs hired by ranchers who wanted their land, and defending the Brazilian rain forest from predatory harvesting by timber barons. She died reciting the Beatitudes.

These modern-day prophets rattled Big Power in the cause of Justice, and paid the price for Costly Love.

The prophet's single-hearted path
Prophets' hearts are so shaped by Love and the urgency of Truth that they are *impelled* to speak out against all that mars, depletes, or destroys the life-giving potency within every person, every living being, and the potential for the good within just systems.

Prophets are passionate about the sacred, the righteous, the good, and *therefore* they cry out against the death-dealing powers that profane, prey upon, enshackle, and crush. Some prophets enter into the dangerous spaces, deliver their prophetic word, and walk away with arrows in their back. Some prophets take arrows straight in the chest, mid-message.

We hear of truth tellers today, often tagged as whistle blowers, disrupters, trouble makers, revealers of dark secrets, who must be silenced, suppressed, removed, exiled, by whatever means. Why? Because their truth telling of the fuller narrative, the real story, the unsettling piece, pulls away the bandages that hide the deep infected social wounds. And Jesus, Prophetic Outlaw, says: "Rejoice! Be glad! For thus they persecuted the prophets before you."

Righteous Outlaws experience a fierce and sober joy, because they know that they can't *not* speak out in the cause of Justice and Truth. The prophet Jeremiah puts it this way:

> I say to myself, I will not mention him.
> I will speak in his name no more.
> But then it becomes like fire burning in my heart,
> imprisoned in my bones.
> (Jeremiah 20:9, NAB)

Righteous Outlaws today, no matter their spiritual tradition, can relate to Jeremiah's interior anguish in the cause of Justice and Costly Love.

If it's so hard, why be a prophet?
Jesus clearly does not act or speak from a place of calculation. He has no illusion of safe outcomes for himself, nor for his followers. He bids them: *Take up your cross* (the Roman Empire's chilling means of executing troublesome outlaws) *and follow me.*

But, you might ask, why be a prophet if I'm going to be silenced, one way or another?

Better to give your life trying, Jesus says with every fiber of his being, than to never try at all. Better to embrace than to suppress the Spirit of the Holy One.

Jesus preached liberation in the midst of an oppressive regime because he *believed with all his heart* that the nonviolent, peace-filled reign of GOD *is possible,* even in the midst of the unfettered reign of Darkness, the sticky grip of King Mammon, the violent reign of Death.

Beatitudes change the paradigm
The Beatitudes are Jesus' condensed vision of ways we *must* live a life of prophetic, creative, positively subversive nonviolent resistance, in right relationship with self, others, Creation, GOD: relationships *shaped* by abiding Peace, *filled* with abiding Peace, and *bearing the fruits* of abiding Peace, especially in the midst of endless oppression, suffering, and death.

The Beatitudes, and the paradigm-changing teachings that follow (see Matthew 5-7), form the core of Jesus' vision of the Land of the Rightside Up. His vision is beautiful, restorative, and just. And his teachings are not easy. Jesus' vision of the Good Way encourages and comforts the afflicted and oppressed, but asks much from the rest of us.

I find it all too easy to "interpret" these teachings, bend them a little, or treat them as negotiable, or "just spiritual," and not really about the complex, gritty here-and-now. But we have only to look at the messes we make, whether in personal interactions and relationships, or in the unjust systems we support through mindless, unquestioning participation in the totalizing regime of King Mammon.

The times we are in, as the times Jesus was in, are ripe for prophetic awakening. *Who will go for us?* the LORD GOD asks. Isaiah responds: *Here I am. Send me!* (see Isaiah 6:8).

Prophets read the signs of the times through the lens of the Gospel

The prophetic dimension of the Gospel is its *corrective vision* of how we must be—individually and as a people—"on Earth, as in Heaven."

I define this prophetic dimension as: "reading the signs of the times through the lens of the Gospel." And not just *reading* but also *acting*—in ways that first of all impel transformation of *my* heart, *my* mind, *my* ways of living which more fully realize the divine vision, here and now.

By *signs of the times* I mean actual evidence of what's going on, what's springing up: Is it Death? or is it Life? Is it divisive? or is it unifying us toward a greater Good? *Reading* the signs of the times asks me to show up, search out, pay attention, notice things, name what I see, discern, and act accordingly. It means *not sleepwalking.*

This way of reading, naming, discerning, and acting asks me to not tune *out* but tune *in*. Such reading, naming, discerning, and acting are vital qualities of the prophet.

Through the lens of the Gospel means to see as Jesus sees, and to follow the way of the Teacher, the costly and inconvenient way of willing vulnerability, as the prophets and witnesses of old did, as prophets and witnesses continue to do today.

The lens of the Gospel makes clear the depths of darkness, abandonment, and death, the trail of tears to the cold and silent tomb. The lens of the Gospel also makes clear the ways of liberating Justice, reconciling Peace, and merciful Love, enabling the prophet to trust that the hidden Holy One, and not ego, is at work.

And *to act accordingly* means to enter, to descend into, to even harrow, as Jesus did, the depths of darkness, abandonment, the spaces of death, and to liberate what has been enshackled: both oppressors and the oppressed. Yes, this is how you "love your enemy."

But first, purification
Prophets today discover that they *first* must be interiorly changed, purified as Isaiah was, proven true as Jeremiah, if they seek to change anything in their workplace, their community, their culture, their world.

Purification is not something prophets *do*. It is something *done to them,* a purification of heart, mind, attitude, spirit, in readiness for a powerful and open-ended calling. They do not place themselves in the crucible and fire it up. They are *placed in* the crucible, and purified in ways they had not imagined.

Isaiah painfully perceives his need for cleansing before he can take up his call to prophetic service: "I am a man of unclean lips," he cries out, "yet I have seen the LORD GOD." A seraph touches his lips with a live coal, saying: "See, now, your wickedness is removed" (see Isaiah 6:5-7).

Isaiah perceives the need for purification, and a divine messenger carries it out. A live coal to the lips probably was not what Isaiah had in mind.

Signs of the times today
The global poor, most notably and tragically, *are* signs of the times today that we seem unwilling to see, much

less acknowledge, intelligently read, and wholeheartedly respond to with an urgency that meets the magnitude of their suffering. They are not poor by accident, nor by choice, but by the work of intentionally designed predatory global military-industrial-economic systems based on insatiable human greed for outsized wealth and power.

We've normalized the well-crafted systems that exploit the labors of the unwillingly vulnerable to generate extreme wealth for the few and to fund our retirement portfolios. We've unhinged ourselves from our birthright humanity.

The institutional church, at least as I experience it in my North American homeland, seems unable to integrally and prophetically address the root causes of such massive injustice and suffering. To prophetically read, name, discern, and act in the cause of global economic and social justice would require church to undergo a massive and profoundly unsettling conversion of heart, mind, attitude, and teaching, and a deep purification of preaching and practice.

Reclaiming its prophetic voice would require church to shed its trappings of power and enmeshment in the sticky web of King Mammon, retire its "brand," and return to that First Love which shaped, nourished, and fortified its early communities.

But most institutions—political, industrial, financial, religious, or otherwise—being structural containers of entrenched power, cannot honestly imagine purification, much less undergo it. As a result, my church seems to ask nothing of me, not really. Why is this so? I sense that to preach the urgency of a just and radically simpler life based on restorative and transformative justice would mean death to Sunday collections. We seem resigned to worship at the altar of King Mammon.

What happens to the poor happens to GOD, Jesus warns us (see his final parable, Judgment of the Nations, at Matthew 25:31-46). The poor belong at the *center* of our concern, not consigned to the margins, or worse, erased from even there.

More signs of the times
Waves of the global poor fleeing political oppression, social unrest, war, genocide, economic oppression, climate chaos, and more, all are signs of the times. Increasing waves of mass killings, and deaths of desperation, also, are signs of the times.

Collapsing and completely inadequate attention to stressed urban infrastructure and crumbling social systems, yes, these too are signs of the times. Increasing disparities between every form of wealth and every form of poverty all are signs of the times.

These troubling signs are *trying to tell us something*. Broad-scale and seemingly intractable social and creational suffering should be making urgent appeal to our deepest moral instincts.

Yet something is tragically wrong—not first with those who suffer, but with those of us who set the terms of existence, both for ourselves and for those who are not us. Curiously, the myriad engineered forms of human and creational suffering seem to be not our concern.

Except, they are. We urgently need to ask: What might be a prophetic vision here for justice, right relations, peace, and the flourishing of life, in *these* times? Jesus, Prophetic Outlaw, has clearly spoken the vision and the desiring of the hidden Holy One. None of his teaching is hidden from us. All of it is waiting for us to actually believe, embrace, and carry out.

The work of Costly Love

We intuit that hidden Good is at work amid the brokenness and suffering. Our every act of waking up, of conversion of heart, of right action, gives witness to divine Justice, Compassion, Love, and insists that human and creational life is *for something* and carries dignity and potential for meaningful contribution to the commonweal of the planet and the flourishing of all of Life.

What's the one sure way for healing our world? The answer is simple, not complex, within our reach, and within our capacity to act imaginatively, creatively, effectively, generously, and compassionately. The way will always be: Costly Love, in expressions beyond counting.

Technology may hold part of the answer, but Big Tech cannot redeem us from our mess. Financial resources may have some role, too. But transactions for exclusionary economic gain must no longer find purchase. We cannot technologize and financialize our way out of a mess resulting from socially myopic vision, raw greed, and toxic exclusionary privilege.

We know the *magnitude* of the invitation to live this sacred and deeply challenging vision by the *intensity* of the pushback—in our own hearts, habits, and expectations, and also in the pushback of corporations, industries, and those who walk the halls of power and are doing just fine under systems of extraction, exclusion, and self-enrichment which they have designed or inherited and enshrined as legal.

Prophets can do only so much

Are the prophets of today going to change everything that is misguided, socially oppressive, or broken? Jesus didn't in his time. Nor will prophets in our time. Consider civil rights leaders, peacemakers, farmworker organizers, Indigenous water, forest, and land keepers, and countless more who have tried and been taken down, or who have aged out in service to the cause.

Like the prophets of old, Jesus stood firm in his truth: GOD alone is GOD, and GOD is Love—something that Caesar never could claim, and still can't. This firm conviction of the ultimately transformative power of Costly Love is the foundation upon which the prophets of our time *must* build, and give witness to, the Land of the Rightside Up, the Good Road, the reign of GOD. Prophets' work is to be awake, to notice; to get their hearts mixed up with the heart of the Holy One, and to speak Truth to power, *with Love:* for the good of whom or what is crushed, and for those who do the crushing.

Prophets get their hearts mixed up with GOD's heart

Jeremiah wrestles with a prophetic calling he did not choose: *I know not how to speak,* he objects; *I am too young!* (see Jeremiah 1:4-9, at v. 6). Later, in the depths of his vocational crisis (see 20:7-18), he cries out: "You *duped* me, Lord, and I *let* myself be duped." (see v. 7). Jeremiah holds in dynamic tension his resistance and his willing vulnerability, as he carries the prophetic fire in his heart, in his bones (see v. 9).

Interior crisis intertwines with the sobering demands of Costly Love. We can only humbly admit that we don't know how this is going to work out, and then, like Jeremiah, take the next courageous step.

The prophetic spirit carries an urgency. Not anxiety, but urgency. Why? Because the trauma of oppression and injustice wounds those who are *willingly* vulnerable (prophets), those who are *unwillingly* vulnerable (the oppressed), and those who hold the power to wound *as well as* the power to change their ways, roll up their sleeves, become useful, bind up the wounds, and set things right.

What breaks the prophet's heart first breaks the heart of GOD. The prophet not merely sees as GOD sees, but also feels as GOD feels, and therefore understands, down to the very core, the magnitude of the wounds. The prophet yearns for the sacred wholeness (read: holiness) of all of humankind and the healing of all of Creation.

Prophetic heartbreak stirs prophetic anger, which is *always a messenger,* not a rage; a *guide,* not a call to violence or revenge. The message? There is an injustice here that needs to be set right for the oppressed, and that also unshackles and heals those who oppress. Prophetic truth requires both courage and humility to speak what is necessary, and always compassionately, with Love, in this place and time.

This man Jesus lived, felt, and wept with a man's heart, a human heart like yours, like mine. He noticed, paid attention, and responded with Costly Love. *He shows us how it's done.*

Living the prophetic lifestyle
For us, to *be like Jesus* means, yes, to go where he goes, and to love whom and what he loves. And it means something more. To *be like Jesus* means to embrace the prophetic lifestyle, where every dimension of your life points to and reveals the good, just, whole, and beautiful vision, the Land of the Rightside Up, now.

The prophetic lifestyle creatively, compassionately, and nonviolently *resists* the consumer culture, the culture of convenience, of privilege, and "power over," no matter where you stand in the hierarchy of economic worth.

The bar Jesus sets seems so high. Yet he shows us, through his ways of showing up in *his* place and time, how we too must show up in *our* place and time. Creative, compassionate *nonviolent resistance* to violence is an expression of prophetic living. Nonviolent resistance does not *argue* with violence, but *remains disarmed and steadfast in witness to Peace*. This is what it means to live as Jesus lived. Such prophetic witness can be done only as an expression of Costly Love.

The prophet's work is not merely to be an irritant to what is wrong (sand in the oyster), but to be a living witness of a better way (a Pearl of great price).

With all my heart I want a world that works for *everyone*. I want the liberation of the poor and *unwillingly* vulnerable who are oppressed by systems that keep them poor, inadequately housed or unhoused; excluded, deprived of opportunity; exhausted, hungry, ill.

And with all my heart I want the liberation of the *well-to-do and powerful*. I want them set free to live their one precious life justly and generously, not for tax write-offs or naming rights, but for the sheer goodness of living their authentic personhood in solidarity with the personhood of everyone else. This is the powerful beauty of restorative, transformative Justice.

Of course, these are heartfelt words, expressing the aspirations of many. But one day I discovered how miserably I, and we, have failed to act on them.

A story: "Remembering Mama Carrie"[23]

Chances are good you've never met Carrie.

But then again, maybe you have.

Maybe you have seen the profoundly sad face, the discolored skin, the washed-out eyes. Maybe you have come close to her exhaustion.

Maybe you have touched her leathery hand. I have.

I'm walking downtown in the noon hour on a Sunday. I feel full of the joy of eucharist. My backpack is full of another kind of holy bread—fresh baked bannock, neatly sliced into fresh-ground peanut butter sandwiches.

In the block ahead of me, on East 12th Avenue, near White Bird Clinic, I espy a woman sitting on the pavement, her back resting against a white picket fence.

I approach. She stares straight ahead.

I gently position myself in front of her, fix my eyes on her eyes, pull the earbuds from my ears, and gently lean down toward her face.

"How are you doing today?" I ask.

She turns her face away from me, and with a dismissive wave of the hand snorts a dismissive reply.

I look at her with love, my heart aching for the broken shard of Humanity before me.

"How are you doing today?" I ask again, gently.

She looks at me from the corner of her eye, understanding, perhaps, that I mean what I am asking, and that I am not going away.

"I baked some bread this morning," I say, "and I have some whole wheat sandwiches with fresh-ground peanut butter in my backpack."

---

[23] A live version of this story appears on my YouTube channel.

I feel pretty certain that she is not expecting this conversation.

"Would you like a sandwich?" I ask hopefully.

Well, OK. Yes, she says, with a tone of reluctance.

I slip off my backpack and unzip the front pouch. And I reach out my arm toward her with the promised sandwich. She reaches up her arm to receive it.

And *in this instant* we notice the beautiful and unexpected.

"Well looky there," she says, coming alive. She points to her left wrist, then to my right wrist.

Her left wrist, with six *copper* filigree bracelets, my right wrist, with six *silver* filigree bracelets.

"Hey, we're sisters," she says.

"My name is Maria," I say. Maria is my street name.

"My name is Carrie," she says.

Sisters, indeed! My heart breaks open with joy. I think hers does, too.

And now today I see, on the front page of my Sunday newspaper, above the fold, a photo of my newfound sister, and an article about Carrie's tragic death. On the front porch of White Bird Clinic. In near-freezing winter temps.

Carrie. Gone.

"She needed shelter ... and we failed her," the caption reads above a photo of "Mama Carrie," famously known and beloved within my town's homeless community. And in the police community, too, it turns out.

"Legalize Survival," a hand-painted sign reads above her tent in the famous unauthorized Whoville homeless camp photo.

> Someone who knew Carrie and the complex burden of sorrow that she bore says to the reporter, "She needed shelter. She needed basic shelter, and we failed her."
>
> *We failed her.* Did I fail Carrie? No, this person speaking to the reporter says: *We* failed her.
>
> Not Big Government. Not labyrinthine systems. We—*we*—failed her. We, who benefit from Big Government and know how to navigate and work these huge labyrinthine systems, failed her.
>
> My people failed Humanity in one of its most fragile and exposed forms. My people failed the test, at least in this one tragic, scarred, and uniquely beloved expression of Humanity.

Is there something I could have done to shelter my sister from the storm of homelessness and raw-edged vulnerability? I want to say *No*. But I know that the answer, also, in some ways, is *Yes*. The prophetic Spirit was there. Where was I? There but also absent? Afraid to mobilize the prophetic agency I already possess?

There are many more Mama Carries in my town. There are Mama Carries in your town, too. Maybe we can be ready at all times, or at least at some times, to share a sandwich, a little time, a little "real presence" of kinship and compassion.

Maybe we can be ready at all times, or at least some times, to show up, speak up, and join with others to press with all our might for social good amidst a sea of social indifference.

We can be ready at all times, or at least some times, to be surprised—by kinship with the oppressed and the invitations of others who walk the Good Road.

And surprised in these ways, maybe we can press our prophetic agency a little farther into the halls of power, get a seat at the table, or bring our own chair; enter the difficult conversations, or begin them if we must.

The takeaway

This story of Mama Carrie is a snapshot of one devastating dimension of a pervasive, dispassionate, well-calculated economic crisis, which strips unwillingly vulnerable people of shelter, dignity, opportunity, hope, and life, to the financial benefit of those who set the terms.

Carrie Miller served in the U.S. Navy Reserves. She was an artist and jewelry maker. She had a mother who now was grieving her loss; she had community. Living with severe physical pain, Carrie's first disability check arrived at last, shortly before she died.

This is the prophetic work of Gospel vulnerability: to show up, notice, discern, name what you see, care enough to accompany, speak Truth to power, always with Love, challenge the sluggish systems that always have their reasons, and invite those who run those systems into a better way.

The assignment

Ask yourself: What unjust political, economic, or social systems are at work in my state? my town? Who suffers? In what ways? Make a list.

And ask yourself: What creative, collaborative, nonviolent prophetic piece might be mine to take on, in Love, to transform unjust systems? What networks are already in place? What am I already doing? What stories can I share?

In Part 6 we explore Gospel vulnerability and the mission of Costly Love.

Part 6

Gospel Vulnerability and the Mission of Costly Love

*On the night he was handed over, he took bread,
and after he gave thanks, he broke it,
gave it to them, and said: This is my body which is for you.
Do this in remembrance of me.*

see 1 Corinthians 11:23-24

Part 5 presented a deeper look at the prophetic dimensions of Gospel Vulnerability, and explored what might be asked of you and me in the cause of life-restoring Justice.

In Part 6 we explore what is asked of us in the mission of Costly Love.

At Passover table on the night of his arrest, Jesus speaks radically, and yes, positively subversive words to those in his intimate circle. How sly the Teacher, the Prophet, on his mission of Costly Love, who knows his time is rapidly closing in.

As though said in a hushed tone, as though the soldiers are at the door, as though there's no time to waste, as though this one last act *must* be done, he says: *Take this, all of you, and eat it: This is my body, given for you.*

Caesar can't say these words. He's not giving over his body, nor one iota of his power. Shedding no blood of his own, he has no qualms about ordering the shedding of blood of noncitizen rabble-rousers, in order to maintain the image of Pax Romana.

Jesus' mission never was to dismantle the reign of *Pax Romana* but to reveal the enduring later-named reign of *Pax Christi,* through his witness of Costly Love.

A way of living "with all my heart"
Costly Love is every action of self poured out into the bread of our commitments, the sacred cup of our lives gladly shared. We express Costly Love in our many ways of showing up *wholeheartedly,* our many forms of inconvenient, intentional, self-giving service.

Self poured out, expressed in these ways, renders sacred everything from the mundane to the dangerous. Everything becomes an invitation into the unseen yet very real presence of the Divine. When I give away a part of myself, I create space for something new.

Be like Jesus
To *be like Jesus* is to *put on the mind of Christ,* to let go personal opinions, personal preferences, personal convenience, personal safety, in service to a far greater cause: the mission of Costly Love for the healing of the world and the flourishing of Life. Where to start?

"Love one another," the Teacher says. *Be* Love for one another, so that when *you* show up, Love enters the room.

Love one another, he insists, including the stinkers who betray you as well as those who love you first, best, and always. He is at such pains to make clear the urgency to love that he makes it a command, which we brush off at our peril. Why?

Because it's never *us* loving one another. It is Jesus himself, cleverly disguised, Costly Love poured out, who loves and yearns to love even more, to love in the particulars, here and now, *in* us, and *through* us. Costly Love is not selective, not conditional. It's inclusive, all embracing. All the time. Always. It's the way of the deeply, consistently, and very present nonviolent heart.

Expect the Teacher to teach you

"It was *not* you who chose me," Jesus says to his closest companions—to you and to me. "It was I who chose you" (John 15:16). *Get that straight,* he seems to say. We were selected to undergo a curriculum we knew nothing about. Not really. We have been chosen to "go and bear fruit that will remain" (v. 16).

To really *understand* Jesus is to let yourself be challenged, stretched, *transformed* by the demands of Costly Love, made uniquely and utterly new in the divine image. I mean Costly Love most powerfully expressed in the healings and teachings, the unsettling prophetic presence, the arrest, trial, death by crucifixion, the burial, and yet more unsettling resurrection of Jesus of Nazareth, holy, righteous, prophetic Outlaw. He shows us just how far Costly Love is willing to go.

Costly Love: More than instinct

I'm pretty sure my mother was willing to risk her life to pull me from the lake when I had slipped underwater. For Jesus, this willingness was not merely instinctive; it reveals his intentional, steadfast way of being deeply rooted in the divine Mystery we call Love.

Jesus *remains* the *living presence* of Costly Love, poured out today through the holy ones, you and me, whether we think we know him or not, can name him or not, whether we even consider ourselves holy or not.

There are no expressions of Love apart from the One who *is* Costly Love personified.

I mean Love powerful enough to break the will to war; Love which cuts through deeply engrained patterns of violence and domination and injustice of any and every sort.

I mean Love which is the healing of the nations; healing of intractable gang violence, tribal rivalries, civil wars; healing of blood feuds, of blood lust for land, resources, profits.

I mean Love that penetrates everywhere, especially into the most hidden and most needful places.

I mean Love that disarms me of my many forms of interior armor, rendering me vulnerable to Love's purifying action. I mean Love that holds open a space for grace and good to have their way for the compassionate inclusion of each and every one in the circle of Life, the yearned-for Beloved Community.

The cost of letting yourself be inconvenienced
Am I willing to be *inconvenienced*—not persecuted but merely *inconvenienced*—by someone, whether family member, friend, or stranger, who needs something from me of far less value than my life?

Well, I might have to think about it, weigh the pros and cons. Will it fit in my schedule? Will it cost me financially? Who are these needy people, anyway? Why are they calling on me? Can't they fend for themselves?

I think of the many Gospel accounts of Jesus feeding the multitudes. These people have been with him, listening to him for a few days, and they're hungry. The account in Mark's Gospel (6:34-44) shows us how easily *we disciples* can excuse ourselves from the humane and challenging tasks before us.

I imagine Mark's text going in a fresh direction. I call it The Multiplication of Love.[24]

> When it's getting late we suggest to Jesus that the crowds be dismissed so they can go into the local villages to get something to eat. But the logistics of Love don't work that way.
>
> *"You* give them some Love," Jesus replies.
>
> At that we say, "Are we going to spend two hundred days' wages for Love to feed them?"
>
> "How much Love do you have?" Jesus asks. "Go and see."
>
> When we figure out how much Love we have, we answer, "this much." He tells us to make the people sit down on the green grass.
>
> Then, taking the little bit of Love that we have gathered, Jesus raises his eyes to heaven, pronounces the blessing, breaks the Love, and gives it to us to distribute.
>
> People feed themselves on Love until they have their fill. We gather up enough Love to fill twelve baskets. Those who have feasted on Love numbered five thousand.

The opening lines of the First Letter of John make clear that the Word *became flesh* in order to communicate, in hearable, visible, touchable ways, this divine Mystery of Love (see 1 John 1:1-4).

The message? *Give some of yourself away,* and you will not be diminished, because there is infinitely more to you—infinitely more to Love—than you realize.

---

[24] This piece appears in *Living as Jesus Taught,* and as a spoken-word track on my *album of the same title*.

Costly Love is sacrificial, generous, willing
I think of the wise desert elder, training timid disciples who want to learn how to *be like Jesus*. "We practice all our little disciplines," they eagerly report, "and say all our little prayers."

The elder grows restless with their little imaginations, and rises up, extending hands, fingers, all pointing upward toward the heavens like dancing lamps of fire, and exclaims with a gleam in the eye: *Why not become all flame?*

Why not become all flame, indeed, utterly consumed in the dancing Fire of Love itself. The cost is not the point. Love is the point: for *this* one, *these* others, *this* worthy cause which merits my wholehearted response.

At his final Passover supper, Jesus willingly sacrifices his *status as Teacher*. He removes his garment of rabbinic authority and ties a servant's towel around his waist *to wash his followers' feet* (see John 13:1-5, esp. v. 4).

He willingly sacrifices his *name* by not resisting the humiliating inscription tacked to the cross on which he is stretched: JESUS, THE KING OF THE JEWS (see Matthew 27:37; Mark 15:26).

He willingly sacrifices his *reputation* as Beloved One by submitting to an unjust public execution, crucified between two revolutionaries for resisting Caesar's rule: a failed messiah, a laughingstock.

Costly Love asks everything of you
Costly Love will ask of you more than you think you have to give from your complex, sometimes difficult and challenging life.

Costly Love will prompt you to step farther, dig deeper, trust more courageously than you are comfortable doing. It will require you to step willingly onto uncertain surfaces, into spaces of vulnerability, as Jesus did, for the good of those whose lives you touch.

Costly Love may interrupt the flow of your day, perhaps even the flow of your life. It will change you, chisel away the parts that are not-you, to call forth the *authentic* You, as Michelangelo did when creating his masterpiece *David.* Costly Love will expand you toward expressions of deep presence, compassion, justice, generosity, and joy, for the good of others, sometimes for complete strangers.

Here's a snapshot of Costly Love in one of those ordinary, close-in hidden spaces.

A story: "My Street Name is Maria"[25]

Early on in my new carfree life I meet Gonzalo.

Gonzalo speaks only the most threadlike English, woven into the sturdy fabric of his Spanish. And I speak no Spanish. So, we strike up a friendship.

"My name is Maria," I say, knowing that he will never master my real name. And I am hoping to learn his name, but do not want to ask.

¿Sí? he says. *Me llamo Gonzalo.*

"Gonzalo!" I say. I make awkward efforts toward conversation.

I notice the morning sun splashing across his warm-toned skin, shining full on his face."Gonzalo," I say, "you … are … beautiful!" He beams.

"May I give you a hug?" I ask.

---

[25] The audio track version is on my spoken-word album *Free to Be Free.*

Gonzalo is in a wheelchair. I think his vision is poor.

So he reaches his arms up toward me, as I bend toward him. He hugs me and hugs me, the way a child hugs the mother. He hugs as though he has not hugged in ... decades.

I mean, who would hug someone like Gonzalo, confined to a wheelchair? I think he might live at the Mission, and I am pretty sure he has no family nearby.

Now I see Gonzalo intermittently, on one street corner or another, or at the transit mall, under the maple trees on the sidewalk in front of St. Mary's downtown. Always in his wheelchair. It never occurs to me to wonder *why* he is in a wheelchair.

Until one warm afternoon, when I am running late for a coffee appointment. And here is Gonzalo sitting in the shade beside the library. Maybe he won't see me, I think, trying to assuage my suddenly discomforted conscience.

I hurry past him.

And my heart is convicted.

I stop short, turn around, and quickly retrace my steps.

"Gonzalo!" I say.

His arms reach up, because I am the mother who loves him. He trusts a mother's love.

And in an instant I understand why Gonzalo lives in a wheelchair. His cutoff jeans reveal a prosthetic leg.

Dear GOD, I groan inwardly.

And I think of all the doors that do not open when you are missing a leg, a limb. And when everything about you says that you are not from here.

And for the ten seconds of our hug I forget about my rush to get to my coffee appointment.

I owe Gonzalo *this gift of real presence* because he is now one of my downtown peeps. And when he hears my voice he knows that he is not cast aside but real, at least in the eyes of his friend Maria.

The takeaway

Costly Love is missional, intentional, deeply self-defining always a fresh revelation of the reign of GOD, like the merchant who finds the Pearl of great price, *and is ready to pay for it.* Costly Love will cost you something, which you discover you are ready to gladly pay.

The burden of Costly Love, I discover, is the burden of getting out of my bubble, of being inconvenienced; a burden I might easily run from. But then I discover: I cannot run. Not really. Nor do I want to. This Love, which is larger than me, has already made its claim on me.

The assignment

Take a few moments to recognize and acknowledge how you *already* express Costly Love. Ask yourself: What is this experience, or commitment, like for me? How would I describe it?

And ask yourself: What story comes to mind? How might I shape it? With whom might I share it?

That's your assignment.

In Part 7 I'll share with you four repeatable steps to actually live Gospel vulnerability and a life of Costly Love.

Part 7

Practical Steps to Living Gospel Vulnerability

We've explored the deeper invitations: to actually live as Jesus taught. Our actions may look different from his, but spring from the same hidden yet dynamic source: a fully embraced vulnerability, always in service to Costly Love.

How to get there? And where to start? I offer you four repeatable steps—a pattern of ways to be present to your world, as Jesus was to his.

Living the *willingly* vulnerable life in solidarity with or for the good of others may be instinctive for you, no matter your spiritual path, something you take as a habit, a way you consistently show up in your world.

Or, you may feel that in *this* circumstance, in *this* new and unexpected turn of events, you *have* no choice, so you give your best, with patience and good intention, to embrace a situation in life that you did not seek.

But how do you find the pattern, develop the practice, and actually *achieve* the willingly vulnerable life?

The key discipline and its fruits

Eat the Gospels daily! Dorothy Day would urge her fellow Catholic Workers; go passage by passage, speaking aloud one phrase or word, one image, at a time. *Hear* the words of this Jesus, revolutionary of the heart. *Embed* them in your heart's memory. Allow the words ample time to settle in and speak to your heart and imagination. Take as your model the prophet Jeremiah, who says:

> When I found your words, I devoured them,
> > they became my joy and the happiness of my heart,
> Because I bore your name,
> > O LORD, GOD of hosts. (Jeremiah 15:16, NAB)

The Apostle Paul writes: *Let the Word of GOD, rich as it is, dwell in you* (see Colossians 3:16). This "dwelling," in time, bears fruit.

The late Archbishop Desmond Tutu had an immediate and lasting effect on me when he described his practice. "I'm a very busy man," I recall him saying, with his signature laughter. "On my especially busy days I allow *extra* time for prayer."

Of course! I immediately adopted this practice, rising often at 11:30 p.m for *extra* unrushed prayer before leaving at 3:15 a.m. for an early flight and two days of teaching. Never once did I feel fatigued.

What might you actually *look* like when you are living such a life? What is the sequence, the flow, from "showing up" to taking action that is loving, just, compassionate, even prophetic?

Four steps to a life of Gospel vulnerability:
The key to Costly Love

I offer you these four repeatable steps, which describe the type of activity, the focus of that activity, and why it matters. You may find yourself taking all four steps within the span of a minute or less, in a given situation. Here's a visual snapshot of the process, followed by fuller text descriptions.

PART 7 | PRACTICAL STEPS TO LIVING GOSPEL VULNERABILITY

Step 1	**Show up and notice what's going on**
Kind of activity	A *Human* activity
Focus of the activity	On *my* world
Why it matters	When you show up, you give GOD *something* to work with

Step 2	**Discern GOD's Love in the situation**
Kind of activity	A *Gospel* activity
Focus of the activity	On the world of *others*
Why it matters	Love must be the starting point of everything, *everything*

Step 3	**Purify your attitude and motives**
Kind of activity	A *Disciple* ("learner") activity
Focus of the activity	Interior preparation
Why it matters	Ego has no useful place in the work of Costly Love

Step 4	**Get out of the boat**
Kind of activity	An *Apostle* ("one who is sent") activity
Focus of the activity	An outward positive action
Why it matters	Revealing what is *new* in the shell of the old is the point of the assignment

Let's explore these four steps in more depth.

Step 1: Show up and notice what's going on

If you want to *live* as Jesus lived, you have to show up and notice what in the world, in *your* world, is going on: in some initial measure, yes, through the reporter's lens, but more importantly, through the lens of this Jesus and his teaching.

Notice, in what you see, hear, read, observe, what consistently tugs at your heart, or sparks your concern. *Notice what stirs your moral intuitions.* Notice what consistently knocks at the door of your conscience.

This is the tug, or the gentle tap, of the Spirit. Which means: It's time, *right now,* to pay attention. Because what tugs at *you,* sparks *your* concern, and stirs *you* to action, actually stirs *your gifts and abilities to respond in a wholehearted way.*

For example: This way of engaging with my world was the context for noticing, and encountering, my friends Mama Carrie and Gonzalo. I showed up in the normal course of my day, and there they were, each waiting for what they could not name: encounter with someone who saw them, who acknowledged them, and made space for them in a lonely world.

And I'll be honest with you. I intentionally underwent a lifestyle change toward more responsive living when I gave away my car some years before these encounters, so that I could trade the security of my motorized bubble for the vulnerability of encountering people on the bus, on the street, who are not just like me, and whose most pressing concerns are far more urgent than mine.

Letting go of my car, and choosing to not replace it, was my courageous, pivotal, no-turning-back commitment to showing up. I undertook it not on a whim but in response to an irrefutable interior calling: *Be among my people.*

Showing up is a Human activity, which requires me to be physically present to my world, and intentionally willing to actually *notice* what's going on. It frees me to ask: Where is the need? where the suffering? the pain? Locally, where are the places where I need to be present?

What might be the unexpected invitation I need to receive, in order to experience "something new" (see Isaiah 43:19).

It's on me to respond with an intentional presence of Love, or at least with compassionate and open curiosity.

The focus in this first step is on *my* world, especially the parts of it that I would not necessarily notice, or intentionally take time to notice, or even *want* to notice, because, frankly, it's inconvenient to notice some things.

Showing up matters tremendously, and for two reasons. First, in our distracted, hurry-up culture, we live mostly somewhere else—in our phones, in our past, in our future. Mostly we're just not here. So showing up is a profound statement about the spiritual importance you place on the here-and-now. Showing up is *incarnational,* which means: intention becomes enfleshed.

And second, the reign of GOD, or the Land of the Rightside Up, is built not by GOD "answering prayers" but by people like you and me showing up, and taking the risk of noticing what's really going on—helpfully through a Gospel lens. *We* become the enfleshed answer to our prayers.

Step 2: Discern GOD's Love in the situation
In order to act in the cause of Costly Love, I must discern GOD's Love—not my opinion or judgment or reasons for resistance—in the situation. Which means remembering always that in the divine plan, Costly Love is the source, foundation, and final fruit of everything. *Everything.* If it's not about Love, it's not about the ways of the hidden Holy One.

To discern means to see, to "read"—here, through a Gospel lens—what's really going on. It means to cut away the excess, in order to find the kernel, the root, the essence, the heart of the matter. I can't rise up to act in a meaningful way if I don't discern the injustice, the broken piece, the suffering, the unjust vulnerability that already moves the divine heart in the situation.

Short of discerning, it's just me diving into a situation —perhaps well-intentioned, but likely clueless about the magnitude of the invitation in the presence of what is at stake.

Discerning GOD's Love in the situation is a Gospel activity, because it stretches me, extends my boundaries out to wider horizons, and changes me, in the cause of Costly Love, as only the Teacher's challenge can.

Discerning GOD's Love in *any* situation is the simplest way I know to get the ego self out of the center of action, and make room for the Spirit, which comes as a tremendous relief. This *letting go and making room* is the real work of Gospel vulnerability—the willingness to be wounded, to have the heart rearranged, in the cause of Costly Love.

The focus in this second step is on the *other*, *this* other, *these* others, who are not me, yet are connected to me through our shared humanity. Which means: Costly Love is *always* connected to life-giving Justice which defends the dignity and rights of those whose humanity is passively withheld, diminished, or actively stripped from them.

Jesus brings life-restoring justice repeatedly, in his ways of being present to others, his healings, his teaching. Our work is to "lean into the heart of divine Mystery," as

Jesus did, in order to see as GOD sees, and to love as GOD loves.

Thinking back to Mama Carrie, I might say, "She's a mess" (for all the reasons I imagine) "and I am not" (also, for all the reasons I imagine). Yet to Jesus she is "sister," and "beloved," the subject and the object of his merciful Love. And in this moment, *his only way to touch her is through me.*

Discerning GOD's Love matters tremendously in the work of rising up to act because discernment keeps my in-charge ego self from moving directly to the solutions I think will "fix the problem." Discerning GOD's Love allows me to step back, move from head to heart, and get my interior self in harmony with the attitude and actions of the Teacher.

What I discover is that divine compassion *always* is with the one who is wounded or broken: whether that's the forsaken one on the sidewalk, the armed and angry one at the mall, the worker on the shop floor, or the executive in the C-suite.

More importantly, this Love is the starting point, the middle, and end point of everything that *is,* in every dimension of Creation, whether at the outermost reaches of deep space or at the very core of human existence. It helps tremendously, I discover, when I remember this, and set my heart and mind accordingly.

Step 3: Purify your attitude and motives
In order to rise up to act in Costly Love, I must do the humbling and sometimes wrenching work of purifying my attitude and motives. I have to purify the rational side of myself which leads the ego to believe that it has something important to contribute here. I have to purify—let *go*—the

part of me that's quick to plan, quick to speak up, quick to judge.

I remind myself that I am not the rescuer here; I am not the savior. I see a situation, sure. But honestly, I don't know how it will play out. I admit my vulnerability. I have the *ability* to act, to respond, in one way or another. But the Spirit must guide me. Which means: Attitude and motives have no place here, other than "the attitude which is Christ's," as Paul insists, and the only worthy motive which is Costly Love.

I think of my experiences with Gonzalo, and Mama Carrie; with the woman in a wheelchair trapped in a scuffle, and with my friend Jorge, also in a wheelchair; with Nina who's falling apart on the bus, and with the barefoot Sock Sister who simply wants to board the bus; with the three bros on the back steps at Safeway, taking it easy on a Sunday morning.[26]

I had to set aside the notion that I had something helpful to offer any of them, and just go with the flow of being led. This is the work of courageous heartfelt trust, and the essence of Gospel vulnerability.

Purifying your attitude and motives, therefore, is a Disciple activity, a learning experience, preparing you for the real work of rising up to act in service to Costly Love.

Discipleship is an ongoing learning, the ongoing refinement of your forms of apprenticeship to the Teacher. Purifying your attitude and motives is the *interior* work of naming and cleaning up those inner forces that keep you from seeing, feeling, and acting as GOD sees, feels, and acts in this world, *through* you.

---

[26] These stories appear in my book *Living as Jesus Taught*.

The focus in this third step is on interior preparation. And I'll be honest with you: The day *will never come* when you are fully prepared, when you will know everything you need to know in order to live in the ways of Costly Love.

You learn on the job, apprentice in the moment, as you take *this* one courageous step, and then the next.

Purifying your attitude and motives matters tremendously, because of Jesus' great love for *this* one, for *these* others. He sends someone he believes he can count on, to stand—with love, compassion, and justice—in his place. That would be you; that would be me.

Don't seek the security of "enough experience," or an assurance that you're being "useful." You don't need to know *how* this experience is going to progress or end. You need only to be willing to be inconvenienced, stretched, and yes, sometimes even wounded in your service to others. You *will* be a witness of Costly Love—yes, perhaps through "useful" activities. Honesty and humility will guide you, as they guided Jesus. Lean wholeheartedly into the assignment, as he did, in humble trust.

Step 4: Get out of the boat
If I want to live in service to Costly Love, I have to actually get out of the boat, when the invitation is issued, as Peter did when Jesus said to him: *Come!*

Move, already! this fourth step says. Getting out of the boat impels me to shift from *intellectual activity* (learning *about* Jesus, believing *in* Jesus) to *willing, wholehearted availability* (actually *believing* Jesus and standing, with courage and humility, in his place).

Getting out of the boat requires me to step decisively from the safety of discipleship *(I'm just a volunteer)* to the raw-edged vulnerability of apostleship *(My wholehearted presence matters)*. I can't just turn away, pretending I didn't notice.

For two winters I ignored the public service announcements calling for "volunteers" to serve at the warming centers for unhoused folks in my town. "I'm so glad my town has warming centers!" I remember thinking. But I didn't hear the plea. *You must be talking to someone else,* I unthinkingly presumed. Until one day I realized: *You're talking to me!*

The next winter, when the invitation arrived, I signed up, got trained, showed up for duty, and I have *never looked back.* That was nine winters ago. At every activation I encounter Jesus cleverly disguised as a shivering woman coming in from the cold, a hungry man devouring a bowl of steamy thick stew; Jesus cleverly disguised as an exhausted person blanketed in deep sleep. And I have encountered Jesus cleverly disguised as a shift mate compassionately deescalating a tense situation, kneeling to change leg wound dressings, bathrooming a paralytic guest.

Getting out of the boat, then, is an Apostle activity. It's the work of one who is sent. It's the natural and powerful outcome of the three earlier steps.

If I want to find and follow Jesus, I have to meet him where he is—somewhere in the shadows, somewhere on the Good Road—and then go where he goes, in order to love whom and what he loves. This, I discover, is what it means to follow Jesus, Teacher, Holy Outlaw to the core.

It's not complex. Challenging? Yes. But I'll be honest with you: Getting out of your particular boat, at Jesus' particular invitation, is the real witness you give to Costly Love, and to the power and beauty of the Land of the Rightside Up.

The focus in this fourth step is positive, outward, reign-of-GOD action. It's the just and compassionate action that invites you into Gospel vulnerability in service to Costly Love. It will expose you to the possibility of being wounded, and it will reveal in this moment, this encounter, a fresh inbreaking of the reign of GOD. In the midst of what is *wrong,* you reveal what is *right, good, and just.*

Getting out of the boat matters tremendously, because it is your contribution to building the Land of the Rightside Up, here and now, in the *midst* of the Land of the Upside Down.

Your family and friends may not understand you. Living a life of getting out of the boat, after all, rocks the boat, sometimes destabilizing close relationships. Family and friends may fear for your safety. Family and friends may fear that you're getting too close to those invitations they try hard to avoid.

Gospel vulnerability, *willing* vulnerability, is vulnerability nonetheless. None of us is bullet-proof. Jesus himself speaks of the Narrow Gate, the Narrow Road, the Good Road that leads to Life (see Matthew 7:13-14). He would know. Trust the Teacher, whose life in its totality is our curriculum.

Closing Words

Why Gospel Vulnerability Matters in Our World Today

We cannot escape, ignore, or even forget what was from the beginning, writes John, Keeper of the sacred Memory:

> what we have heard,
> what we have seen with our eyes,
> what we looked upon
> and touched with our hands.
> (1 John 1:1, NAB)

We cannot ignore the inescapable truth of this man Jesus: Teacher, Prophet, Healer, Lover, and as early church boldly proclaims, crucified Lord, and risen Christ. Willing vulnerability remains the core of his witness and the golden thread which runs through and unites all four of the Gospels.

Caesar Augustus issued plenty of "gospels"—his means of spreading the "good news" (read: conquests) of Empire. Yet his gospels were no match for the utterly new —and for Caesar, utterly troubling—inbreaking of the reign of GOD—on his watch, within his empire.

A gospel *devoid* of the radically good news of divine inclusive justice, nonviolence, generosity, and joy, which Jesus preached with his life, is no gospel at all. Still, we're slow to understand, slow to wholeheartedly give ourselves, our lives, to such a radically life-restoring vision.

The many forms of oppression that infest every part of society in every part of the world seem to multiply like cancers in the body. Violence gets us nowhere. War doesn't work. We know this. Division tears us apart and drains us of our agency for a shared and greater good.

While greed is actively killing us, our culture tells us that backing away from such a totalizing regime marks us as uncool, no fun, losers.

Yet I speak from my heart: The world, whether it knows it or not, desperately *needs* you and me, each and together, to come forward, step up to the moment, and dare to *believe* that creative, intentional, inclusively *nonviolent engagement* in the cause of humanity and all of Creation is more effective than armoring up for more violence in the race for domination.

The world begs us, whether it knows it or not, to hold open a space for something better, quieter, more humane; a space for life-restoring Justice, and disarmed and abiding Peace.

In John's Gospel the Evangelist boldly affirms from the start:

> The light shines in the darkness,
> and the darkness has not overcome it.
> (John 1:5, NAB)

In our time, Light *does* shine in the darkness, and the darkness violently insists that, through whatever means necessary, the Light must go away.

As eye witness to the Teacher's crucifixion, death, and burial, John has seen up close the forces of darkness. And in the dark and empty tomb he witnesses the unexplainable inbreaking of Light.

CLOSING WORDS | WHY GOSPEL VULNERABILITY MATTERS TODAY

Today Jesus, the Willingly Vulnerable One, Teacher, Prophet, Healer, Lover, Righteous Outlaw, crucified Lord and risen Christ, asks you, asks me: Are you willing to go *with* me, to stand on my behalf, in places of darkness, oppression, poverty, exhaustion, and the many forms of dying, in order to *draw close* to the suffering, and to *be* my Justice, Mercy, and Peace?

He asks us: Are you willing to walk in the footsteps of prophets, witnesses, and all the unnamed holy ones who have gone before you to be a living presence of Costly Love? Are you willing to stand together, steadfast and strong, and never back away?

Yes? Shall we go?

Be courageous. Love the community that feeds you and holds you secure. Drink from the pure sources. You know them when you find them—or when they find you.

Those who have gone before us in courage, humility, and radical trust, and those yet to come, urge us on at every step as we choose the beautiful, vulnerable path of Costly Love.

About the Author

Essayist, storyteller, and public theologian Mary Sharon Moore is passionate about helping individuals to claim their deeper purpose, and inviting communities into thoughtful, constructive, nonviolent conversation on issues of justice, peacemaking, and social and creational good.

She also serves as spiritual guide to individuals nationwide who are committed to social justice and an intentionally nonviolent lifestyle.

Mary Sharon believes that every day, every activity, every moment, is a fresh invitation to enter wholeheartedly into the hidden yet very present Holy Mystery, whom she calls GOD.

Mary Sharon's books, spoken-word albums, and videos offer fresh and compelling language for those seeking insight, worthy action, and deeper meaning—antidotes to the hurry-up scan-and-scroll world.

marysharonmoore.com

A word from the author ...

If this book has been meaningful to you, *please,* purchase copies for friends! Spread the word! As an independent writer I rely on readers like you to help me share the fruits of my labors.

When you order from my website, you support my work directly.

Or, request copies from your local independent bookseller.

To schedule me for your next event, or to receive an author-direct bulk discount on six or more copies of any of my titles, please email: connect@marysharonmoore.com

Made in United States
Troutdale, OR
03/03/2025